Garland Studies in Historical Demography

Stuart Bruchey

Allan Nevins Professor Emeritus
American Economic History
Columbia University

GENERAL EDITOR

A Garland Series

International Migration and Population Homeostasis

An Historical Study

David L. Elliott

GARLAND PUBLISHING, INC.
New York London
1989

Library of Congress Cataloging-in-Publication Data

International migration and population homeostasis : an historical study / David L. Elliott.
p. cm. — (Garland studies in historical demography)
Thesis (Ph. D.)—University of Oregon, 1984.
Includes bibliographical references.
ISBN 0-82405092-4 (alk. paper)
1. Labor mobility—History. 2. Alien labor—History. 3. Emigration and immigration—
Social aspects—History. 4. Emigration and immigration—Economic aspects—History.
5. Population—Social aspects—History. 6. Population—Economic aspects—History.
I. Title. II. Series.
HD5717.E55 1990
304.6—dc20   89-77118

Printed on acid-free 250-year-life paper

Manufactured in the United States of America

ACKNOWLEDGEMENTS

The data utilized in this thesis were made available in part by the Inter-university Consortium for Political and Social Research. The <u>Cross-National</u> <u>Time-Series</u> <u>Data Archive</u> was originally collected by Arthur S. Banks. Neither the collector of the data nor the Consortium bears any responsibility for the analyses or interpretations presented here.

I would like to thank my wife, Eveline, for her support through the course of this study. I must acknowledge the invaluable advise given me by the members of my thesis committee: Dr. Lawrence Carter, Chair; Dr. Albert Szymanski; Dr. Vallon Burris; and Dr. Cheyney Ryan. In addition, Dr. Patricia Gwartney-Gibbs was kind enough to read a draft of the proposal and has given me useful advise at that time and since.

TABLE OF CONTENTS

LIST OF TABLES

LIST OF FIGURES

CHAPTER I

INTRODUCTION

The Problem: International Labor Migration

International migration presents a number of important
social issues to many countries. While flight from
political repression, ethnic oppression, or religious
persecution has been a motivating factor for many migrants,
the economic motivation to migrate often underlies such
seemingly evident reasons. Historically, the economic
motivation has sent traders, caravans, shippers, and
plunderers across the globe. The same motive is
responsible for the massive forced migrations of slaves and
indentured workers. Some population movements, often of
entire communities or nations, have been constituted by
settlers in the search for land. In the capitalist epoch,
the migration of free workers seeking employment has been
paramount. This study, however, is not immediately
concerned with individual motivation.

This study focuses on underlying demographic,
environmental, and socio-economic factors which encourage

international migration as an institution. By "migration" I refer to the movement of human beings from one place of residence to another. But I am also speaking of migration as an institutionalized phenomenon characterized by social patterns of occurrence, not simply a random movement of individuals across territorial space. By "social patterns" I am speaking especially of migration streams, an assemblage of migrants having, over a period of time, common origins and destinations.

The socio-economic consequences facing countries of emigration and immigration alike may lead to serious internal conflicts and they may also contribute to fundamental structural changes within the affected societies. These consequences of international migration may include distortions of age and sex compositions of the populations, remittances and related international capital flows, problems of education, unemployment, ethnic and cultural antagonisms, and spatial inconsistencies in labor and/or "human capital" supply and demand. Spatial inconsistencies are often associated with uneven national or regional development. Any of these issues, directly or indirectly, may lead to political unrest. As I see it, the central problem in the present conjuncture, one which reflects both uneven development and which causes political unrest in a number of countries, is the territorial inconsistencies in the distribution of cheap labor and investment capital. The territorial inconsistencies are both a national problem (for some countries) and an international problem which is often "resolved" by the flight of capital to areas with cheap labor or the migration of laborers to areas with a relative abundance of jobs. Migration as a resolution of the problem, however, leaves intact the territorial and class inequities in ownership and control of economic processes and may merely intensify the existing uneven development. Political conflict which arises from the problem of uneven development, therefore, may be postponed to a later date.

My belief is that in order to understand the present issues and problems surrounding international labor migration, one must gain an understanding of both the structural setting within which social and economic activity take place and the historical processes from which concrete contemporary problems and issues are derived. The present study of migration and the transition from feudalism to capitalism represents an attempt to reach some understanding of the structures and historical processes which have helped create and shape international labor migration, and the issues and problems associated with it. This study is carried out by developing a structural problematic which is joined to the historical processes

associated with migration and the transition to capitalism.
The task is accomplished by following a series of
hypotheses[1] designed to explain a number of concrete
historical problems and issues in light of the problematic.
The inquiry is essentially exploritory and the hypotheses
are "working hypotheses" as opposed to "formal hypotheses"
designed for operational tests. An overview of the scope
and content of the present study may best be had by a
preview of the contents of the chapters which follow.

Chapter Outline

Chapter Two

The second chapter consists of a review of important
theoretical perspectives on migration referred to in this
work. I address the following theoretical perspectives:
the push-pull perspective, Ravenstein's laws of migration,
and the economic and historical demography school
represented most prominently by the National Bureau of
Economic Reserch (NBER).

---

[1] See chapter four for a list of these hypotheses.

Chapter Three

Chapter three details the problematic: the articulation of Wrigley's homeostatic model with a Marxian historical periodization. What I essentially argue is that population parameters--mainly fertility, mortality, and migration--operate to maintain population size within certain homeostatic limits, the latter determined jointly by environmental and socio-economic factors. The relative importance of this mixture of factors varies greatly and is not open to a priori determination. In general terms, I suggest that in earlier historical periods, environment seemed to have a greater impact upon population size while in modern times, the social structure would seem to have a greater impact. I argue neither for nor against the possibility that a reversal in this general trend could take place. My main interest is with the socio-economic factors. Among them, I see the mode of production as having overall paramount importance.

Mode of production and historical periodization are discussed in some detail. Included are discussions of the productive forces and the social relations of production as abstract categories from which an understanding of the concept of the mode of production may be derived. The historical periodization I propose, a modification of

Marx's, includes the primitive communal epoch; the pre-capitalist epoch (consisting of the advanced communal, the slave, the petty commodity, and feudal modes of production); and the capitalist epoch which is commonly divided into the competitive/industrial phase and the monopoly/imperialist phase. I then discuss the concept of structural discord and economic development. Structural discord is the abstract, theoretical explanation for the apparent stagnation or underdevelopment of certain countries when two (or more) disharmonious modes of production co-exist such that the social relations of one and the productive forces of the other dominate the society. Structural discord results in the social relations constricting the development of the productive forces causing a systemic stagnation.

Chapter Four

The fourth chapter addresses methodological issues. First I discuss historical sociology as the methodological foundation of this study. I see "methodology" as neither method nor theory but as the intellectual means by which the two are joined. Next I address specific historical methods as the means by which the raw material of history is gathered and made available. The main historical methods my sources and I have drawn upon to extract from

various types of historical evidence the actual historical
processes include social history, economic history,
historical geography, and historical demography. I then
address time series analysis, a statistical method by which
data so derived may be analysed. A discussion of the
various units of analysis--community, nation, and
world--follows.

The chapter closes with a list of working hypotheses
informed by knowledge of the historical processes but
derived from the structural logic of the problematic.
These hypotheses are designed to explain in terms of the
homeostatic model, certain problems and issues of migration
during the transition to capitalism. These problems and
issues are outlined in the following preview of chapters.

Chapter Five

Chapter five begins the historical analysis and there
appears here a marked shift in the level of discussion,
from relatively abstract in the previous chapters to
relatively concrete in the fifth and succeeding chapters.
In chapter five, I survey the population setting,
particularly the types of migration prevailing, on the eve
of the fourteenth century population crisis. Focusing
mainly on Britain, as is the case for the subsequent four
chapters as well because Britain was the birthplace of

modern capitalism, I demonstrate the interconnection between the feudal social structure and migration.

It is common knowledge that the middle ages was a period in which wandering minstrels, preachers, peddlers, and other individuals attached neither to land nor lord were to be found. The medieval migrants who were structurally antecedent to contemporary migrant workers engaged in corporate migration: mass movements or redistributions of population. Corporate migrations--waste land settlement and conquering invasions--are discussed in the context of the feudal social structure. I also discuss the role of traditional corporate forms of migration in the collapse of feudal society.

Chapter Six

This chapter addresses population movement in England after the population crisis of the fourteenth century. In particular, I address population trends, the emergent class formation of English cities, and state intervention into migration processes.

I discuss the structural change in class formation associated with the population crisis and the role of state intervention in maintaining population homeostasis. The homeostatic implications of structural change for the re-growth and redistribution of population which preceeded the emergence of capitalism are introduced.

One important question of historical demography is the issue of the prolonged population stagnation after the onset of the fourteenth century population crisis. In light of the homeostatic model, I examine the reasons for the failure of population to return to the pre-plague level as might be expected by a strictly demographic reading of the homeostasis hypothesis.

The issue of the emergence of London and the general redistribution of population from rural areas to cities is addresed. I suggest that important structural changes took place in the rural feudal economy which released a latent reserve population which in turn fuelled the process of urbanization.

Chapter Seven

Chapter seven consists of a survey-analysis of the English class structure in the period immediately prior to the English bourgeois revolution. While population issues are not addressed in a substantive way, it is necessary to develop a class analysis of this particular period of English history in order that hypotheses designed to explain subsequent developments which affected both migration and economy may be understood.

Chapter Eight

This chapter addresses population, economic, and
environmental questions raised by the inflationary period
Europe experienced in the sixteenth century. The primary
means by which feudal population homeostasis is maintained
through the interaction of such demographic variables as
migration, marriage, household composition, etc., is
examined.

Another issue analysed is the impact of demographic
factors on the European economy of the sixteenth century as
an antecedent of the seventeenth century European crisis.
In particular, I address both the impact of colonial
treasure and the impact of rural population growth upon the
sixteenth century price revolution.

An apparent fall in mortality and general increase in
the population of Europe are addressed in the context of
environmental factors. This transformation relates to the
"demographic transition," an essentially descriptive
perspective on population growth which may be explained
theoretically by means of the homeostatic model which I
utilize.

Chapter Nine

Chapter nine addresses the colonization of the Americas by European powers specifically as a population issue. A structural analysis of the European economy in the colonial period is utilized to shed light on the reasons for the various forms of colonization and colonial labor organization. Colonization and colonial labor are seen as important determinants of the subsequent patterns of international labor migration and capitalist development in the Americas.

Chapter Ten

Chapter ten represents another shift in the focus of the study. Whereas chapters two through four are somewhat more theoretical and abstract, and chapters five through nine are more oriented toward Britain, chapters ten and eleven analyse immigration to the United States from seven European countries. Not only does the geographical focus shift, but methodologically I move from a qualitative historical to a quantitative historical analysis.

Chapter ten consists of a preliminary data analysis of trans-Atlantic labor migration in the free trade period of capitalism. In this chapter I develop time series models designed to demonstrate the working of the homeostasis model in the context of international labor migration.

Unfortunately, satisfactory environmental variables could not be developed so the analysis concentrates upon population and economic factors. The aim of this chapter is to determine which specific independent variables are statistically significantly[2] associated with the dependent variables which are measures of the rates of migration from Belgium, Denmark, France, The Netherlands, Spain, Switzerland and the United Kingdom to the United States. The discovery of the significant independent variables is then passed on to the next chapter where further data analysis of multivariate models is conducted.

Chapter Eleven

Chapter eleven continues the data analysis begun in chapter ten and is oriented toward specifying and explaining the unique set of independent variables which are correlated with migration from each of the above countries to the United States. Previous analyses of European migration to the U.S. in the industrial capitalist period have demonstrated the importance of the American economy as a "pull" factor upon potential European emigrants. The main question I address here is: what

---

[2] Henceforth, unless otherwise stated, when I speak of "significance" in the context of a data analysis I refer to statistical significance, not significance in the more substantive sense.

other economic and population factors are operating and
what are their effects upon trans-Atlantic migration, both
over time and among countries?

Chapter Twelve

The final chapter summarizes the results of the
analysis and reviews the ability of the homeostatic model
to suggest viable hypotheses to explain specific historical
demographic issues.

CHAPTER II

MIGRATION THEORIES

The subjects of demographic research--the aggregated social and natural events associated with birth, death, and (to a lesser extent) population movement--lend themselves readily to analysis by the "scientific method" because of their regular and universal occurrences. What is surprising, given this character of demographic events, is not that demographic studies tend to be empirical and descriptive, but that no coherent demographic theory designed to explain fertility, mortality, and migration has found general usage.

As with demography in general, attempts to develop migration theories (perhaps except those regarding urbanization) are usually more descriptive than analytical.[3] The main theories which influenced this study are outlined in this chapter.

---

[3] This view is supported by others such as Shaw (1975) or Mangalam and Schwarzweller (1970).

Push-Pull

If there is any standard perspective or model of migration it must be the "push-pull" paradigm or framework. This is in large part because its eclectic nature (see Bogue's 1969: 753-754 summary) lends itself to various theoretical orientations. This approach suggests that people migrate because they are pushed from their place of origin and/or pulled to their destination. The push-pull approach may be useful because it allows for non-demographic causal variables: political, economic, and social psychological factors often having been cited as push factors, economic factors as pull factors. However, it is hardly a theory in itself and in the final analysis, it falls victim to Petersen's (1969) critique.

Peterson argues that the push-pull approach assumes the essential sedentary nature of human society. Obviously such an approach cannot explain nomadic societies, the very existence of which calls into question the fundamental assumption which is implicit in the push-pull approach. While the explicit or implicit identification of "push" and "pull" factors may well be an important element of many migration studies, the inference is that migration possesses physical properties similar to polarization within a magnetic field. The present study, while

eschewing the magnetic analogy, utilizes push and pull as
descriptive categories by which variables derived from
other theories are classified.[4]

The Laws of Migration

One of the foundations of migration studies is the
classical example of inductive theory by E.G. Ravenstein
(1885; 1889). In Ravenstein's first article, he analysed
the census returns of the United Kingdom attempting to find
patterns of migration based upon one's place of residence
vis-a-vis one's place of birth. He distinguished between
localities of "dispersion" or net out-migration and
"absorption," localities of net in-migration. Ravenstein
also considered the rate of natural increase (births minus
deaths) in his analysis. In the second article, Ravenstein
attempted to extend his analysis to Europe and North
America insofar as sufficient data were available. The
findings which seemed to be repeated in different

---

[4] It should be mentioned that Petersen has developed a
more elaborate typological alternative designed to meet
the theoretical deficiencies in migration theory. Like
the push-pull, however, Peteresen's typology is also a
system of classification, not a systematic theory and
while it has certain advantages over the push-pull
perspective, it is not directly applicable to the present
study (largely because it does not satisfactorily explain
the historical appearance of the various types of
migration). Nor does it warrant further discussion here
as a leading perspective since it is rarely referenced in
the literature.

countries, Ravenstein declared, were the "Laws of Migration." Those which will be seen to bear most heavily on the present study are summarized below.

Perhaps the most general, but none the less most important observation Ravenstein made was that most migration was seemingly related to job seeking. This observation, in the context of modern capitalist society, is quite compatible with the thesis elaborated in the following pages.

Distance considerations constitute a second set of generalizations on migration. Ravenstein's study of internal migration in a number of countries demonstrated that short-distance migration predominated. For example, in general terms, non-native residents of given localities tended predominantly to be natives of neighboring localities. Ravenstein's theory was that migrants would go to the nearest larger town such that migrants from small towns would go to middle-sized towns and migrants from these middle-sized towns to large ones. While it is true that long distance migration did take place, the migrant typically was said to make his or her way in stages to progressively larger towns until, ultimately, the migrant arrived at one of the "great centres of commerce or industry" (1885: 199).

Ravenstein theorized that international migration followed this general pattern. For example, European immigrants to the United States would be most likely found in the Eastern seaboard cities of industry and commerce. Westward expansion tended to be undertaken by natives of the eastern states rather than European immigrants. Ravenstein's findings based upon census analysis and individual case studies of immigrants to America are genereally in keeping with this theory.

In Ravenstein's analysis of emigration from Southern Europe, he suggested that not only does the distance law seem to hold, but a similar climate also seems to have an impact as North Africa was colonized predominantly by immigrants of French and Italian extraction. In his analysis of international migration, Ravenstein may have revealed an additional factor. He theorized that the amount of arable land seems to help determine the countries of dispersion and absorption. Perhaps related to this was Ravenstein's finding that rural peoples seemed to be more migratory than residents of towns. Finally, Ravenstein discovered the existence of "counter currents" of migration: return migration to one's place of origin followed patterns similar to the main currents but in distinctly diminished numbers.

Ravenstein's laws--which might better be described as
a set of generalized observations and findings, and
theoretical explanations for them--have probably had a
greater impact upon subsequent migration researchers than
any other single body of theory. Moreover, the method of
census analysis pioneered in part by Ravenstein has also
influenced subsequent researchers. However, there is one
striking deficiency in this method which in turn affects
migration theory development: censuses are usually taken
on a decennial basis and thus the discovery of short-term
factors which influence migration may escape census
analysis. In the past half century, time series analysis
methods have been developed and, when applied to migration
data (e.g. steamship passengers or immigrants admitted),
discovery and exploration of another important theoretical
dimension has opened up. The time series analysis method
will be addresed in the chapter on methodology.

Economic and Historical Demography

The economic approach to historical demography allows
the researcher to bring to bear upon migration studies
theoretical insights of the dismal science. Much of the
work in this field in the United States is associated with
the National Bureau of Economic Research (NBER). Among the
earlier researchers of note, Jerome (1926) and D.S. Thomas

(1927), the latter quite explicitly, operated from an economic deterministic time series varient of the push-pull approach. The shared argument was, essentially, that migration serves to supply labor to areas with relative shortages, the robustness of the labor-short economy determining the immigrant cohort size measured by time interval (e.g. year or quarter). According to Jerome (1926: 88), "particularly after the Civil War, the cyclical fluctuations in immigration are to a large extent a reflex of industrial conditions in the United states, the effect upon immigration evidently becoming apparent in something less than a year."

Another important development in economic and historical demography, especially in relation to trans-Atlantic migration, was the concurrent publication of Kuznets and Rubin's Immigration and the Foreign Born (1954) and the first edition of Brinley Thomas's Migration and Economic Growth (1954). Other important related works from the NBER school which appeared in the wake of Kuznets and Rubin (1954) include Kuznets (1961), Abramovitz (1964), and Easterlin (1968).

Kuznets and Rubin expanded the theoretical scope of the field and made important empirical and methodological contributions as well--the latter best exemplified by their development of the concept of an apparent twenty-year cycle

in migration and economy (subsequently dubbed the Kuznets
cycle.)

While Kuznets virtually redefined the theory and
methods of research on migration and economic cycles, two
additional researchers have made significant theoretical
and empirical contributions following the pioneering work
of Kuznets.

The British scholar, Brinley Thomas,[5] has made
important contributions to the specific topic of cyclic
economic and migration patterns in a study which focuses
upon British migration to the United States but which
considers more peripherally other migration streams.
Thomas, like most members of the NBER School, associates
migration with such economic measures as residential and
railway construction. These he sees as measures of the
economic draw of the United States upon European
population.

Citing the nineteenth century studies of the Swedish
demographer G. Sundbarg, Thomas traces the Kuznets cycle,
at least in part, to twenty-year cycles in the excess of
births over deaths in Europe (Thomas, 1973: 157). Brinley
Thomas's primary concern is with the corresponding cyclic
patterns among economic and demographic variables.

---

[5] The references hereinafter are to the second,
revised 1973 edition of Thomas (1954).

According to Thomas (1973: 33), the Kuznets cycles,

> showing an average interval of about eighteen
> years from peak to peak, suggest two hypotheses.
> First, it is possible that agricultural society
> has experienced a Malthusian cycle involving a
> regular recurrence of extreme population
> pressure; Scandinavian vital statistics, which
> are unbroken from the early part of the
> eighteenth century, lend colour to this view. As
> soon as the development of transport had made it
> physically possible for large numbers of people
> to cross the ocean, it would be natural to expect
> heavy emigration to occur in those phases of the
> demographic cycle when there was relative
> over-population. Secondly, a considerable inflow
> of migrants into a new country must exercise an
> important influence on methods of production.
> Since these inflows occur in periodic waves, they
> might be the cause of minor secular changes in
> manufacturing technique. For example, the growth
> of mass production in the United States may have
> passed through qualitative phases induced by the
> long fluctuations in immigration.

The suggestion is, therefore, that the cycles of natural

increase are the result of previous episodes of high

mortality. In periods of low mortality, emigration

increases.

The NBER researcher and Kuznets associate, Richard

Easterlin (1968), has contributed additional insight into

the Kuznets cycle. Easterlin is not centrally concered

with migration, certainly not before 1870. Easterlin

mainly affirms the existence of twenty-year cycles in

immigration and demonstrates what he believes is the

economic implication of this to the United States. More

importantly, Easterlin acknowledges that the immigration

cycles seem to have ceased at about the time of the Second
World War while the twenty-year cyclic patterns in economic
variables have persisted. Moreover, according to Easterlin
(1968: 10, note deleted):

> In the period since 1940, the demographic
> movements have exhibited some striking
> differences from the earlier pattern. Previously
> the component of change principally responsible
> for the swings in population, labor force, and
> households was migration, both external and
> internal. Recently, the dominant components of
> change have been, respectively, the birth rate,
> labor force participation rates (particularly of
> older women), and household-headship rates,
> although internal migration too has continued to
> play a part.

The reasoning is that age-specific population increases
(whether due to immigration or an earlier birth rate
increase) cause rises in the numbers of households
established, which in turn has extended economic effects in
the context of demands for goods and services. In other
words, a temporary, short-term phenomenon such as an
episode of net in-migration due to factors in another
country or region, or a surge in the the post-war,
post-depression birth rate, would set up a situation in
which the number of young adults and the number of
newly-formed households would increase. This would
establish a long-term demand for food, clothing, schools,
consumer goods, etc. which tends to maintain economic
growth. In current terminology, this would be a
demand-side as opposed to a supply-side argument.

Kuznets and followers represent the leading theoretical perspective in the historical and economic analysis of trans-Atlantic migration. Their collective insights into the interconnection of migration with other population factors and economic growth cannot be ignored.

Population Homeostasis

Another important theoretical orientation from which, however, implications for migration must be inferred, is the homeostatic model as elaborated by Wrigley (1969). The central feature of the homeostatic population hypothesis is that demographic parameters act to maintain a stable population at an optimum size given the established environmental and socio-economic setting.[6] The optimum population size would be found within a range between a minimum and maximum of what might be called a "carrying capacity."

Population size which departs from the carrying capacity would require, for the maintenance of the society, fundamental changes in either the environment or the social structure. As population size departs from the optimum and approaches the limits of the carrying capacity, survival of

---

[6] The homeostatic hypothesis or model, especially as developed in the following chapter, is an elaboration of that proposed by Wrigley (1969). Wrigley did not focus centrally upon migration, which is my primary contribution to the development of the homeostatic model.

the society would depend upon demographic correction or the process of social or environmental change which would alter homeostasis. This alteration of homeostasis could take place incrementally but at certain points, for reasons which must be determined by concrete analysis, a fundamental restructuring of society and environment would be necessary. By "homeostasis" I refer to the complex of carrying capacity and optimum size as established by the articulation of social structure with environment.

Within the three elements of the homeostatic model are several particularly salient factors. Under "population," fertility, mortality, and population movement are the parameters immediately responsible for maintaining population size. Under "environment," access to arable land, energy resources, weather, and epidemic disease act upon the population parameters. By "socio-economic," I refer to social structure in the broad sense of customs, values, and norms; government and politics; and economy. There is a virtually limitless complex of interactions among these (and related) factors.

Population Factors

Fertility and mortality are fairly straight-forward. Increases in fertility and decreases in mortality, with no migration, will increase the size of the population.

Decreases in fertility and increases in mortality under the same conditions would have the opposite effect. If the model were that simple, homeostasis would be maintained solely by compensatory changes in fertility and mortality when, for some exogenous reason, one deviates from the level which maintains homeostasis. This is probably the most fundamental dynamic operating within the homeostasic model. However, as a homeostatic corrective parameter, fertilty (for example) does not change on its own. It requires some alteration in community social behavior. This behavioral change may be as drastic as infanticide (which effectively, though not technically, reduces fertility), or as subtle as a slight change in the age of first marriage. In either case, the changed behavior is caused by material conditions of population becoming incompatible with homeostasis and appears as changes in social norms and values.

Within the context of various environmental and socio-economic conditions, different communities will have different population carrying capacities. When extra-demographic changes take place which alter either the actual population size, the carrying capacity, or the optimum population size of a territorial unit,[7] net in-

---

[7] The territorial units of analysis utilized--community, nation, world--are discussed in chapter four.

or out-migration may take place. Such migration among territories serves to either supply or absorb population of a territory which, for some reason, has either deviated from homeostasis or experienced a change in homeostasis.

The operation of these demographic factors may be illustrated by reference to environmental changes which, themselves, shall then be discussed in more detail. Let us say that, all other conditions remaining stable, environmental factors may change such that the death rate of a community is altered. Examples cited in the following chapters include unfavorable weather causing crop failure or rodent infestation causing epidemics. In either case the death rate rises and population size tends to decrease. Moreover, historical evidence indicates that fertility rate changes may reinforce mortality changes under some environmental conditions. For example, in medieval periods of food shortage, deaths rose and births fell while during plague epidemics, "the number of births held up surprisingly well" (Wrigley, 1969: 115). As the death rate fell with the return of an adequate food supply, according to the homeostatic hypothesis, births would increase sufficiently to restore the population to its previous level (Wrigley, 1969: 113).

Suppose that temporary environmental conditions were to be localized, developing positively in some communities

and negatively in others. Such a pattern would suggest
that some communities tend to experience overall population
increases and others decreases. According to the
homeostatic hypothesis, environmental or socio-economic
factors, acting through mortality, migration, or fertility,
would be expected to intervene. The crop failure example
illustrates this. With the return of adequate food
supplies, postponed marriages and conceptions would push
the birth rate to a temporary high while mortality would
reach a temporary low as malnutrition had eliminated the
weak and sick from the population--those who would have
constituted the highest mortality risk group for subsequent
years.

Regarding another historical type of depopulation, it
is likely that the onset of the plague not only raised the
death rate, but stimulated flight from the affected
community. Wrigley's (1969: 115) sixteenth and
seventeenth century data suggest that urban in-migration
increased following the passing of disease as the lost
population was replaced. The homeostatic hypothesis
suggests that community population size would tend to
return to the level existing prior to the environmental
intervention, assuming no fundamental socio-econonic
change. Population size, itself, would be determined by
the specific combination of environmental conditions and

socio-economic factors which act upon fertility, mortality, and migration.

Environmental Factors

Some environmental factors, especially climate and geography which together determine the arableness of land, are relatively permanent and may be seen as constant factors which help to determine the carrying capacity of a territory. Weather and disease organisms may have more transitory influence upon the size of a population. Access to energy is meaningful only in the context of the prevailing technology.

Weather and disease generally are seen to act upon population through mortality, though at a later point I shall note some of the other effects of these usually transitory factors. By changing the immediate conditions of life, weather and disease could be direct causes of migration. By changing the size of the actual population, they could affect migration indirectly, in that migration could be one means by which population could return to its original level. In the following chapters I shall point to several instances in which such environmental factors had both direct and indirect affects upon migration.

A change in climate may have been a factor which contributed to the fourteenth century population crisis. In the capitalist period, however, I do not see climate--a stable environmental factor--as an immediate condition of change but must note the relatively short-term and virtually random shock effect of adverse weather on the agricultural economy: temporary departures from the seasonal norm. Imlah (1958: 162, 167, 169) makes it clear that even as late as the last quarter of the nineteenth century, English weather affected harvests which in turn affected international trade.

  The earth's surface contains approximately 30 billion acres of ice-free land area but only about one-fourth is potentially arable. However, much of this potentially arable land would require irrigation or other pre-cultivation works to make it ready for farming. The potential for cultivation is determined by two factors: soil and climate (President's Science Advisory Committee, 1967, Vol. II: Chapter 7). However, as of the late 1960s, less than half the earth's potentially arable land was actually under cultivation. The best explanation for this, given the persistent hunger in some parts of the world, is that under the capitalist system, the investment required to bring much of the remaining land under cultivation is more profitably utilized in other economic sectors since the most fertile land has long been cultivated. At any rate, it is clear that even today, arable land remains a requisite of industrialization--though this is not necessarily correlated on a country-to-country basis.

Another important environmental factor which had special impact upon the industrial revolution, and countries where the industrial revolution first took hold, was endowment with fossil fuel reserves. Without coal or an alternative energy source which could replace and multiply human and animal energy as a factor of production, the industrial revolution could never have taken place. While other energy sources had a long history of use: wind and water power; the burning of wood, charcoal, or peat--only coal had the property to provide the heat necessary for the emerging metallurgical technologies. Not only that, but coal (once the steam engine was put into service) was a more reliable and transportable source of mill power than any other, at least until petroleum came into use. The latter did not begin to appear in sufficient quantity until the late 1800s. Knowledge of how to utilize energy resources and access to them represent important determinants of a society's economic conditions. Access to energy, in the context of prevailing technology, is seen as an indirect influence upon migration, operating through the economy.

In summary, for the post-feudal period, three main environmental factors are salient: fossile fuel reserves, arable land, and weather. We now understand that at the present rate of use, neither fossil fuel reserves nor available land are inexhaustable.

Social Structure

One must be aware of the danger of reducing the argument to one of environmental or demographic determinism. It is suggested here that of the three major factors--environment, population, socio-economic--changes which appeared in any, without self-correction, would be expected to cause adaptive changes in one or both of the others. If the homeostasis hypothesis is valid, and since environmental factors are known to change, we must also assume the mutability of social or economic factors.

While the population factors are clearly related to migration, within the homeostatic hypothesis I see them as "dependent variables" in the sense that they maintain the existing population size, changing only when extra-population forces act directly upon them or when population homeostasis, itself, changes.

The social structure consists of independent variables. I conceptualize the social structural variables in the context of three categories: culture, state, and economy. Culture consists of customs, values, and norms of the society, whether the "society" be local, regional, national, or transnational. Specific data values of population variables may be determined by the culture prevailing within the territory undergoing concrete analysis. Reference to the state suggests that political and governmental actions may intervene, directly or indirectly, in the population process. The economy refers to the means by which labor power and means of production are brought together to assure the material subsistence of society.

Culture

The primary importance of culture is probably the set of customs and mores which determine the rate of fertility. Key elements within this would be marriage and contraceptive practices. Social norms regarding age at first marriage and post-partum abstinence are traditionaly important factors which determine the birth rate of a society. The prevailing type of family and household composition are important contributing determinants of fertility but they also bear upon migration. In societies where there is great inter-generational dependence, there is likely to be relatively little long-distance migration which separates the dependent family members from the economically active--unless the economy has developed sufficient means by which subsistance may be provided from a distance.

State Intervention

State intervention into population size may be direct
and intentional, direct and unintentional, or indirect.
Examples of direct and intententional intervention would be
efforts to curb fertility by encouraging the use of
contraceptives. A usually unintentional (but as I shall
point out in a subsequent chapter, not always so), direct
intervention into population size would be warfare.
Indirect state intervention into population size would
include policies which have the effect of providing
economic security for older citizens, security which was
formerly provided by the extended family. Should the
economic need for a large family diminish over time, the
argument is that family size would tend to decrease.

With regard to migration, state intevention will prove
to be a key factor in the following chapters. I will
illustrate the means by which population has been forcibly
redistributed, both within some countries and
internationally, directly by the state or with the state's
support. The state may also restrict population movement
as is common with national immigration laws.

Economy

 I have come to conclude that the single most important factor which determines population size (through its impact upon demographic variables) is the economy. This should be true for migration, especially, among the demographic variables which establish population size. There are innumerable economic variables which, directly or indirectly, affect population in general or migration in particular. These important variables, however, may differ according to the historical, economic period in which they act. Some economic variables important in one period may be relatively unknown in another. An example of such an economic variable would be wage rates. In some historical periods, relatively few members of society depended upon wages for a living. In the current period, wage-earning is the single most important source of income for much of the world and a significant amount of migration is labor migration: workers seeking wages, or higher wages.

Summary

 In this chapter I have outlined the migration perspectives utilized in the present work: the "push-pull" perspective, Ravenstein's laws of migration, and the economic and historical school of demography as it relates

US gets much migration because of our economy, "land of opportunity"

to migration. Perhaps the single most important theoretical significance of this school is the explicit connection between economic growth and international migration, especially migration from Europe to the United States. But not unlike Ravenstein's findings, I believe that the cyclic analyses of such scholars as Thomas (1973), whose work shall form an important staging point for me in a subsequent chapter, may be too historically specific to allow for generalizations across historical periods.

Marxian political economy and the homeostatic model which derives from Wrigley's (1969) historical demography, form the two foundations upon which my thesis has been constructed. While the Marxian analysis, like the Ravenstein and Thomas analyses, is specifically geared toward the capitalist epoch, it is also linked with a body of theory oriented toward analysis of pre-capitalist societies; this is quite unlike Ravenstein and Thomas. Wrigley's work, while not specifically geared toward migration, is intended to span broad historical epochs. Inferences from Wrigley lend important insight into the workings of population, environment, and social structure. In the next chapter, I shall effect the articulation of these two theoretical approaches, Marx's and Wrigley's, to produce a unique and (I believe) fruitful direction from which international labor migration may be analysed. An important component of the problematic which follows is the joining of the demographic theory, which might be said to approach migration through fertility, with an economically-oriented theory which approachs migration from the perspective of labor.

CHAPTER III

THE HISTORICAL PROBLEMATIC

Central to the thesis upon which this study rests is the belief that certain modern social phenomena, like international labor migration, can best be understood by their study and analysis in historical and comparative relief. That is, in order to fully grasp the nature of international labor migration, one must be able to compare its attributes with other forms of migration, particularly those from which it emerged. What makes this not only desirable, but possible, is the belief that history is not to be unravelled like a ball of knotted strings to reveal its component parts neatly lain out, one succeeding another. History is made by a complex of human actors particularly through class struggles. But history also operates within a dynamic of its own, in the sense that certain important events, discoveries, or developments, once they have appeared, leave an indelible mark upon all succeeding epochs. The cultivation of the earth is one such development; use of the wheel is another; discovery of the secret of the atom may be the last. Social developments or patterns of behavior, too, leave their marks.

Historical Materialism: Structure and Process

Historical materialism as a method of analysis is often misunderstood, as much because of ill-prepared analyses purporting to be historical materialist (or simply "Marxist") as because of its uninformed critics. There are two dimensions of historical materialism, both open to misunderstanding: economic determinism and class struggle.

On Structure and Economic Determinism

The single greatest point of misunderstanding (among proponents as well as opponents) is the idea of economic determinism. Historical materialism suggests that in the final analysis economic practices shape the cultural, cognitive, and political practices of a society. But the cultural, cognitive, and political practices cannot be reduced simply to the economic. Nor do economic practices inevitably pre-determine specifics of the others. The human factor, the ability of humans to transcend the limits seemingly placed upon social reality, is ultimately determinative. That is, there can be no mechanical application of social "laws" which limit or determine human behavior. The human factor is what allows for the exception to the laws of social science. Human beings, both as individuals and as social groups (especially social classes) make their own history within the context of, but not necessarily limited by, a legacy of both opportunities and constraints inherited from the economic and social institutions developed in generations past. In the long run, historical meterialism sees the economic legacy as having paramount importance. This does not deny the conjuncturally specific pre-eminence of psychological, political, cultural, environmental, and other factors. But again, in the long run, the constellation of immeasurable and unpredictable extra-economic factors pale in importance compared with the economic.

The most often usual formulation of economic determinism is found in the "base-superstructure" concept. The concept of an economic base or substructure is too often misunderstood to suggest a dichotomy between economic and every other behavior by casual or careless readers of Engels and Marx.[8] It is true that in the final analysis, the economic constraints placed upon social

---

[8] The reader cannot be faulted entirely (Fischer, 1973: chapter six, passim). Historical materialism did not emerge from Marx and Engels' collective intellectual and political endeavors like a bolt of lightening. It developed over the course of their collaborations and isolated references may be misconstrued to suggest a simplistic relationship in which political and other activities are reduced to some economic determinants.

behavior tend to limit the options available, at least in the short run. But a careful reading of concrete analyses of actual conjunctures,[9] demonstrates that a whole series of political and ideological practices may mediate and intercede in the actual workings of society, rendering historical materialism (in careless hands) a matter of faith or (in the hands of its opponents) inadequate and erroneous.

The economy, if I may avoid use of the "base" or "substructure" terminology, is <u>ultimately</u> definitive only in the sense that in the final analysis, human societies must provide themselves with the means of subsistence. Ken Post (1978: 17) writes:[10]

> A fundamental theoretical proposition . . . is that economic practice is indeed the major determinant. First, it provides the material basis of human existence, and that makes it sovereign; man cannot long live by thoughts alone. Second, economic practice is the foundation of the class structure, since it assigns to people their basic roles (slave, master, merchant, clerk, and so on) and through its social relations places them in the process of exploitation (as exploiter, indirect exploiter or indirectly exploited). Third, economic practice provides essential means of production

---

[9] I am thinking here most particularly of Marx's (1973) <u>Class Struggles in France</u> and <u>The Eighteenth Brumaire of Louis Bonaparte</u>.

[10] I must acknowledge the important influence Post had on my earlier attempts to grasp the fundamentals of historical materialism. Post kindly made avaliable to me an earlier draft of portions of the manuscript which was subsequently published and is cited here.

for others, the taxes by which the state . . .
sustains itself, . . . Fourth, the needs of
economic practice at the level of distribution in
particular require forms of state power which, .
. . ensure the concentration of wealth and power
in ways compatible with the continuing domination
of the ruling class.

On Process and Class Struggle

The other dimension of historical materialsim is the

human dimension, the class struggle. Even if the economy

establishes certain limits or constraints upon human

behavior, it does not predestine that behavior. Historical

materialism according to Fischer (1973: 89-90)

is not historical fatalism; it does not exclude
the alternative; from the fact that decisions are
conditioned, it does not deduce that destiny is
unconditional.

Historical materialism takes account of the human factor,

the analysis "always proceeds from social reality, not from

abstract categories" (Fischer, 1973: 91). The social

reality of contradiction figures as a key component of the

historical materialist analysis and this appears most

salient in the social process of class struggles. The goal

of my historical analysis is the revelation of the social

reality of international migration though a formal

statement of theory, methods, and thesis preceeds the

discussion of social reality.

Migration and Historical Materialism

With regard to migration and historical materialism,
the social reality of any conjuncture consists of a complex
of environmental conditions, historically established
normative behavior, and political reality alongside the
material conditions of the production and reproduction of
the society's subsistence. The individual act of migration
is based upon this complex of factors. Only infrequently
is the complex of factors surrounding the individual
migrant available for historical analysis. In the absense
of sufficient raw material for such a case study of
individuals, the approach I take is the analysis of the
social and environmental settings of specific historical
conjunctures. The conjunctures I address in most detail
are: in chapter five, the fourteenth century because of
its profound connection with population retrogression; and
in chapter seven, the seventeenth century because of the
importance of the English bourgeois revolution. Included
within the social reality of these conjunctures would be
some information concerning the extent of migration. By
examining the process of the transition to capitalism from
the vantage point of various conjunctures, the changes in
the patterns of migration vis-a-vis other social and
environmental factors may be discerned. Equally important,

however, is the pattern of continuity from one conjuncture to another. It is this structural continuity within the midst of a series of discontinuous social and economic processes which I have attempted to reveal in the problematic of this study. In a related, but larger sense, I suggest that human society has experienced three major epochs in the period of its existence.

The periodization which I elaborate below derives from Marx's, particularly as articulated in the Grundrisse. It is also an attempt to reflect upon some of the current interpretations by other authors, though entering into detailed debate is beyond the scope the the present study. The three major epochs which form the foundation of my historical analysis include the capitalist (currently), the pre-capitalist, and the primitive-communal.[11] These categories, and their components, are not intended to be rigid, linear stages through which all societies must

[11] Some might choose to add the socialist or communist epoch to this typology. There is a certain logic to this which Marx utilized in the context of the political organization of the working class. For a historical periodization, however, the addition of an epoch which has not fully proved itself is an exercise in teleology. Until such time that some form of socialism comes to dominate the world system, as capitalism has, we must speak of socialism within the context of the capitalist epoch. The social patterns of migration associated with socialism present a series of problems beyond the scope of the present study. Insofar that migration now takes place between socialist and capitalist countries, I think that it can be analysed within the context of the capitalist epoch.

inevitably pass. They derive logically from three fundamental assumptions. I assume, following Marx's demonstration in Capital, that capitalism is qualitatively different than any other economic system and that its first lasting appearance was made in seventeenth century England, marked by the bourgeois revolution. I assume, secondly, that in the evolution of the human species, class society did not exist from the beginning--it emerged at some point in the development of human society. I assume, thirdly, that the emergence of social classes within human society marks a point just as important as that marked by the emergence of capitalism. Therefore, I see two fundamental junctures establishing three broad epochs in the development of human society. The emergence of social classes marks the juncture between the primitive communal and the pre-capitalist epochs; the development of free labor separated from the means of production, and accumulated capital invested productively, mark the juncture between pre-capitalist and capitalist epochs.

For any social system, I assume that there must be some coherent means by which economic production takes place. Economic production, in its most fundamental sense, is the joining together of human labor power with the means of production: raw materials, land, tools, etc. One possible purpose of migration is to effect such a joining.

The transport of tools and materials from the place of
origin to the place of production would be the alternative
to labor migration when labor and the means of production
are spatially separated, though in actual practice most
production will engage elements of both. The transport of
finished products to the place of consumption is the usual
means of joining consumers with the products. Migration as
a population factor can be said to have important economic
implications in the sphere of production rather than
consumption--consumption of a finished product--though in
the larger sense it could be said that there is a
continuous production-consumption-production process.
Since migration may be seen to sustain production by
joining labor with its raw material (including land), it
may also be said to constrain production where migration
forces effect a separation of labor from the means of
production. My own conceptualization is that the "mode of
production" is the abstract, structural dimension within
which the joining of labor with the means of production is
institutionalized. I believe that the mode of production
is also an important concept which helps to distinguish the
major epochs from one another.

Mode of Production

The "mode of production" is a specific combination of
productive forces and social relations of production. The
productive forces of a society correspond to the spheres of
production and consumption while the social relations
correspond to the spheres of distribution and exchange
(Elliott, 1978: 155-56).

Productive Forces: The Spheres of Production and
Consumption

The sphere of production exposes the underlying
property relation between the subject of labor (the worker)
and the object of that labor (the product). Is the product
the property of the worker? The key to this is the
specification of which social class controls the separation
of the product from the producer. For example, under
capitalism, the capitalist owns the means of production and
controls the separation of the product from the producer.
The producer is the non-owner of the product which is
alienated from him or her by its owner; the capitalist has
also purchased the labor time of the producer.

Under what I shall later discuss as "the petty
commodity mode of production," the actual producer owns the
product and sells it for money. The petty commodity
producing class, therefore, controls the alienation of its

own commodities from itself. Under other pre-capitalist modes of production, labor time or actual products may be transfered from the producer to the non-producer by extra-economic means (e.g. feudal obligations).

This distinction is important in an international system. In the pre-capitalist epoch, especially the mercantile period, colonial products (usually raw materials) were not only separated from the producers (e.g. slaves) by extra-economic means but were separated from the place of production by a combination of economic and extra-economic means. International trade under the world capitalist economy, once the colonial vestiges of the pre-capitalist epoch have been discarded, takes place largely without direct political or military intervention into the economic process. Imperialist control of trade in the capitalist epoch, however, utilizes extra-economic means of control hidden within the economic.[12] At the world level, the sphere of production is defined not by the national identity of the products exported but by the national identity of the entity which exerts control over exports--control over the alienation from a nation of its produce.

---

[12] An example of this would be the political "destabalization" of elected governments, such as the Allende administration in Chile, by the United States government.

The sphere of consumption demonstrates the productive or unproductive use to which products are placed. Productive uses include consumption by workers as food and the utilization of raw materials, tools, etc. Unproductive uses include consumption for ceremonial purposes or for the feeding of non-producing classes. The sphere of consumption reflects the mode of production to the degree that the products are utilized productively (thereby maintaining or increasing the productive forces) or non-productively (thereby dissipating the productive forces). Simply said, a continuous production-consumption-production cycle in the pre-capitalist epoch does not necessarily expand, because the surplus is siphoned off for non-productive use by the exploiting class. In the capitalist economy, however, the productive consumption cycle does expand, as much of the surplus accumulated by the exploiting class is consumed in further production rather than being squandered in ostentatious or other non-productive ways.

Regarding the international dimension of consumption, the identification of the consuming nations derives from the concentration of the production-consumption-production cycle in those countries where the internal economic system is better geared toward productive consumption. This is especially evident in the capitalist epoch though the loci of the concentrations of productive consumption depend upon those factors of production which, in combination, yield the greatest profit.

The productive forces of a society are determined jointly by both (1) the class nature of production from which is determined the actual producers' abilities to control the disposal of their products and (2) by the extent of productive consumption. In a pre-class society, the producers would typically control the disposal of their own products and productive consumption would be at a high level--i.e. relatively little non-productive consumption--though not expansive in nature. In a pre-capitalist society, the actual producers would have limited control over the disposal of the product of their work, some non-productive consumption would likely be evident among the members of the ruling class, and over the long term some expansion would likely have taken place. In capitalist society, the workers would typically have no control over the disposal of their products while expansive productive consumption would be under control of the bourgeoise.

Relations of Production: Spheres of Distribution and
Exchange

The spheres of distribution and exchange correspond to
the social relations of production. The sphere of
distribution exposes the class patterns by which the
products are alienated from the producing class in the
sphere of production. In any class society, products as
well as the ownership of the means of production are
distributed inequitably among the social classes such that
one section of society is able to gain a disproportionate
share of the wealth produced by that society. The class
which gains a disproportionate share of the wealth--the
social surplus--is usually a non-producing class: for
example, the bourgeoisie under the capitalist mode of
production. This social surplus may be consumed
unproductively in which case no accumulation takes place;
it may be hoarded or consumed productively, thus enabling
the class which is distributed this surplus to accumulate.
The sphere of distribution, therefore, identifies the
accumulating class.

The accumulated surplus is distributed inequitably not
only among classes but, especially from the colonial period
onward, inequitably among nations. Part of the reason for
this is the uneven distribution of the factors of
production around the world, but as a geo-political problem

the political distribution of factors of production is the
result of historical processes. In the world economy,
therefore, the sphere of distribution identifies the
nations which accumulate wealth. The spatially inequitable
distribution of accumulated wealth, in the capitalist
epoch, tends to reproduce itself through the imperialist
system. The spatial distribution of certain key factors of
production--labor, capital, and land (including natural
resources)--holds the key to the analysis of international
labor migration.

The sphere of exchange derives from the means by which
products are alienated from the producers and distributed
among members of society. By "means" I am refering to the
type of physical substance (or its symbolic form) which
changes hands reciprocally for the product. The means of
exchange may be another product, it may be some utilitarian
item with a generally accepted value (a universal
equivalent), or it could be a form of money or credit with
only symbolic substance. The means of exchange also
defines the prevailing means of accumulation of the
society. For example, where the universal equivalent and
form of accumulation is a product (e.g. beads, gold,
cattle, etc.) hoarding is usually the type of accumulation
which takes place, an accumulation which forstalls
circulation and thus consumption--productive or otherwise.

Where money is accumulated, the possibility of lending the accumulated money in exchange for interest and return of principal presents itself, but not necessarily as capitalist accumulation. Instead, it may be as primitive, mercantilist accumulation. We speak of capitalist accumulation where accumulated money is invested in production by wage labor.

The sphere of exchange may effectively limit the development of the economy and hence act as one factor which establishes the dominant mode of production. For example, where the means by which exchange is conducted is based solely or predominantly on barter or the exchange of goods in kind, wage labor (a prerequisite of capitalism) could not be the norm--the sphere of exchange would thus prevent the operation of an economy based upon the capitalist mode of production. In this sense, and since the means of exchange delimits the means of accumulation, the sphere of exchange is an important determinant of the class nature of society.

On the international plane, the means of exchange is an important determinant of the phase of the international economic system. When specie was the primary means of international exchange and mercantilism the prevailing ideology of trading nations, accumulation of gold took place in those countries best able to plunder others and exploit the other populations to their own advantages. This represented one element of the "primitive accumulation" which preceeded capitalist accumulation. As the mercantilist urge to accumulate precious metal as money gave way to the exchange of commodities and other products,[13] the capitalist countries engaged in productive consumption were able by capitalist means to multiply their economic power and enforce the Ricardian fiction of "comparative advantage" upon the international system thus effectively controlling accumulation on the world scale. However, once exchange was no longer primarily product for product, but mediated by capital, the stage was set for the imperialist phase of the capitalist epoch.

Summary

The productive forces of society, conceptualized within the spheres of production and consumption, are responsible for the rate of expansion of the economy by the extent of productive consumption. The social relations of production demonstrate the class nature by which

---

[13] Emmanuel (1972: xvii) points out that the mercantilists who held to the quantity theory of money advocated the influx of precious metals to increase employment and production. The bourgeoisie, of course, wished to increase commodity production, thus their willingness to import raw materials rather than gold in exchange for manufactured exports.

accumulation and expansion take place. At the international level, the prevailing productive forces and social relations determine the patterns of exploitation of nation by nation and of accumulation among nations.

International labor migration is a moment of the sphere of distribution: the distribution of the factors of production. The conditions of migration (free or unfree) help to indicate the nature of the mode of production dominant within the international system. The direction of migration (the redistribution of factors of production) indicates the nations most actively engaged in productive consumption relative to labor resources, at a given point in time, therefore the location of the most vibrant productive forces.

Homeostasis and Mode of Production

Different modes of production, like different environmental settings, contribute to the establishment of homeostasis--the population carrying capacity and the optimum population size. In a territorial context, this may be measured by population density, though the contribution of environment vis-a-vis social structure in establishing optimum, maximum, and even minimum population sizes cannot be determined by density, alone. What I believe is most crucial and what has direct bearing on migration is the type of economic activity engaged in by the population.

Agriculture, industry, and non-industrial urban trade and manufacture represent three possible types of economic activity. These are generally associated with relative densities of population, agriculture being the least dense, urban economy (industrial or non-industrial) allowing or requiring the greatest density of population. These types of activity are also associated with modes of production. In the capitalist epoch, however, an additional factor of production lends itself to the model and may alter the land-labor relationship.

Capital represents labor of generations past, the "crystallized labor time" contained within means of production which have undergone previous labor processes. Crystallized labor time, as constant capital, may be relatively fixed, as with factory and railway infrastructure, or it may be quite portable as with certain machines and tools. The mobility of capital vis-a-vis labor is an important determinant of labor migration in the capitalist epoch. The mobility of each is determined in part by technology, in part by the stage of industrialization, and in part by the relative strength of labor. Historically, technology has made constant capital more mobile. Transportation has been improved and engineers have reduced the size, weight, and cost of many means of industrial production. In the early stages of industrialization, there was the need to erect industrial sites, highways, railways, housing, etc. which by nature are relatively fixed. In the later stages of industrialization, the established infrastructure has largely been utilized, so long as the marginal utility of the infrastructure in the short run did not warrant rebuilding, except as in (e.g.) Japan or Germany where it was destroyed by war. The relative strength of labor refers to the political ability of organized labor to assure high wages and long-term benefits.

The relative mobility of capital and labor under the industrial capitalist system, therefore, depends upon the marginal utility of existing infrastructure, the cost of transporting the means of production to other locations, and the willingness of labor to move to other locations. The latter depends, in part, upon the relative strength of labor in the different locales. Where workers are paid high wages and feel secure in health and retirement, and when unemployment is low, they would be less likely to move to a place where the relative strength of labor is less.

The more advanced or modern the social structure, the more important would be economy as opposed to environment in establishing patterns of migration. Unless migration has come to have diminished importance vis-a-vis fertility and mortality in the maintenance of homeostasis (which I believe it has not), one must conclude that economy has become relatively more important in establishing and maintaining population homeostasis. No teleological implications for the future roles of economy and environment in homeostasis are intended. If I were to speculate on the future, I would guess that environment may again become the predominant factor--this will likely be detemined by how effectively the people are able to purposefully intervene in the economy-environment nexus.

Historical Periodization

The historical periodization proposed below is intended to join the abstract concept "mode of production" with more concrete features of societal development as it is known or believed to have taken place. In the following paragraphs I address primitive communal, pre-capitalist, and capitalist epochs (and subdivisions within) in the context particularly of migration vis-a-vis surplus population and overpopulation. Let me define "surplus population" as those workers made redundant by economic processes and "overpopulation" as population at or exceeding the homeostatic limits of a society, that is, a greater population than can be supported under existing socio-economic and environmental conditions.

The Primitive Communal Epoch

The primitive communal epoch encompassed human society from its first appearance to that period when distinct social classes could be discerned. The economic systems of this epoch were small-scale and community-oriented: hunters, gatherers, fishers, herders, and the like. Agriculture was rudimentary. Migration in this period probably served mainly to redistribute population over different territories, a requisite of shifting agriculture, nomadism, and similar economic systems. I believe that migration, particularly where it was institutionalized, had an underlying economic function--no matter how obscure it might now appear.

While primitive communalism has characterized human society for much of its exstence, by definition, the internal orders of the primitive communal societies would not long possess the contradictions necessary for the development of class society without undergoing the transition to a pre-capitalist mode of production. Class society could emerge, conceivably, through the domination of one tribe or nation by another. If this is correct, the foremost contradictions of such primitive communal societies could well have arisin from migrations which placed one tribe or nation in competition with another for access to land and other natural resources. Of the many possible consequences of such competition (e.g. amalgamation of the societies, annihilation of one, territioral displacement and emigration of one), the conquest by one and the persistence of multiple cultures could have led to a caste and subsequent class society.

Due to rudimentary development of the economy, it is expected that the environment would be the primary determinant of optimum population size, social structure less so. The argument is that with the social structure held constant, the homeostasis would have a greater tendency to vary according to changing environment while with environment held constant, the homeostasis would vary less, according to changing socio-economic factors, provided the mode of production remained primitive communal. Overpopulation--should it occur--would likely result from environmental as opposed to social structural changes.

This discussion of primitive communal society is highly speculative and general. We probably do not now, nor ever will, possess the knowledge necessary to "test" such a proposition because all that remains of primitive communal societies are isolated and anachronistic groups. And while the primitive communal epoch is not the central concern of the present study, I believe that its logical place within the typology is valid and it is generally in keeping with our knowledge of primitive societies.

The Pre-Capitalist Epoch

The pre-capitalist epoch is intermediate within the typology. It is distinguished from the primitive communal primarily by the existence of social classes. While there is a two-class logic driving the pre-capitalist modes of production, additional social classes may co-exist in specific societies. The pre-capitalist modes of production include the advanced communal, the slave, the feudal, and the petty commodity.[14] Contrary to the more conventional (Stalinist) interpretation of the progression from one mode of production to another, my position is that none of these necessarily follows any other though each occupies a logical position between primitive communal and capitalist society.[15] Let me outline each.

---

[14] This varies somewhat from the pre-capitalist modes of production suggested by Marx (1965). Aside from nomenclature (discussed below), Marx did not propose a "petty commodity mode of production." Marx did, however, suggest the possibility of a "Germanic" mode of production. This is evidently a reference to the effects of the extension of feudalism to Eastern Europe, and in my judgement, not a mode of production, per se.

[15] For example, it is generally understood that slavery preceeded feudalism in Europe though I shall discuss in a subsequent chapter the localized reinstitution of slavery, for a period, at the end of feudalism, during the transition to capitalism.

The Advanced Communal Mode of Production

What I have called the "advanced Communal" is more
commonly known as the "Asiatic mode of production" (AMP), a
name which obscures more than it illuminates.[16] The
advanced communal is characterized by largely
self-sustaining village communities which engage in
socialized production under direction of a national ruling
class whose exploitation of the producing communities is
mediated by the state. The organization of production at
the village level may vary greatly from one society to
another but it is postulated on some economically
significant degree of cooperative labor or some other
socialized form of labor.

The state's legitimacy, (often embodied in the
personage of an absolute monarch--the "Oriental despot"),
is established by virtue of the state's carrying out the
function of organizing production on behalf of the ruling
class. The ruling class, through the legitimacy of the
state, maintains a claim on the producers' labor time

---

[16] Many students of a Marxist orientation toward
pre-capitalist societies have rejected the Asiatic mode
of production as a concept. Perry Anderson (1975) and
Barry Hindress and Paul Hirst (1975; 1977) are currently
the most notable opponents though Bailey and Llobera
(1981) demonstrate that Marxist opposition to Marx's
concept of the AMP is rooted in the Stalin-Trotsky
struggles for power in the Soviet Union, the Stalinists
being opposed to it. The most detailed treatment of the
AMP is found in Krader (1975).

and/or the means of production. Even though this is an exploitive system, with a non-producing class controlling the state's extraction of the surplus labor of the subjects, there is symbolic, if not real, economic reciprocity between state and subject. The state, therefore, performs some economic function essential for the maintenance of the society as it is constituted. The economic function of the state may range from the annual notification of the time for the peasants to plant their crops, to the organization of public works projects which contribute to peasant productivity, irrigation works being the best-known.[17] In exchange for these "services" the ruling class (ostensibly the state, mediated by the state bureaucracy) extracts surplus value from the producing communities.

My own historical studies of Thailand (Elliott, 1978) have demonstrated two major types of migration in the advanced communal epoch. For one, from the fourteenth to

---

[17] The former probably represents a symbolic gesture by the state bureaucracy, rooted in primitive communal times, when community elders through tradition and experience had come to learn the best time to sow. Irrigation works provided long-term stability in water supply in the face of yearly variations in rainfall, thus assuring sufficient harvests even during years of adverse weather. This is a good example of a social institution designed to mitigate the adverse effects of abnormal weather conditions, helping to assure population homeostasis by reducing the threat of drought or flood.

the ninetenth centuries, the entire society as a corporate
unit (including the monarch's place of residence) moved
southward through a portion of Southeast Asia, acquiring
ever more fertile land as the population moved into the
Chao Phraya delta, what is now Central Thailand. Secondly,
as population grew, some peasants moved to the periphery of
the territory ruled by the Thai state. These two migratory
tendencies, over the centuries, operated to expand the land
claimed by the Thai king.

In pre-capitalist Thailand, and this may be true for
many advanced communal countries, there was no threat of
overpopulation due to the presence of vast areas of
uncultivated land. The availablilty of unpopulated land
(aside from some isolated primitive communal tribes) is one
factor that allowed the Thai state to expand through the
centuries. Migration, therefore, was the primary relief
valve for tendencies toward the exceeding of the optimum
population size; migration contributed greatly to the
maintenence of population homeostasis in that the land area
added to the kingdom tended to increase the population
carrying capacity of the territory occupied by Thai
society.

The Slave Mode of Production

Marx (1964) called slavery the "ancient classical" (Greco-Roman) mode of production. The characteristic feature of the slave mode of production is the existence of private property in the forms of both the means of production (land, tools, etc.) and human beings. Slavery has clearly appeared in many different social environments though it can be said to be the dominant mode of production only when the extraction of surplus value through slavery constitutes the primary means by which the ruling slave-owning class gains wealth. The state does not necessarily engage in actual economic activity though due to the nature of slavery, an oppressive state apparatus is required by the ruling class in order to control the labor force.

Due to the inordinate oppressiveness of slavery, it tends to encourage (if not require) migration. On the one hand, the slaves are legal property and disposable. As such, there is a constant demand for their replacement. While one means of replacement is purposeful breeding, the length of the human life cycle makes this an expensive and time-consuming process. Consequently, the capture of both individuals and entire communities and their transfer to another location is an example of (forced) migration.

Slaves also escape, making clandestine migration a feature
of many slave societies. Escape is one means by which
overpopulation is avoided; high mortality, another.
Migration will be seen to constitute an important element
of my analysis of the slave origins of international labor
migration.

The Feudal Mode of Production

Feudalism is characterized above all by serfdom. With
feudalism, a portion of the serf's labor time was privately
appropriated by the lord and served as the primary means of
accumulation by the ruling class. The state is not seen as
directly involved in economic activity; its main roles
being the mediation of conflicts and competition within the
ruling class, the enforcement of feudal laws (generally to
the disadvantage of the peasantry), and the protection of
the society against extra-societal economic and military
threats. The most important form of migration in feudal
Europe was the colonization of unpopulated lands and of
those lands occupied by less powerful neighbors. As
environmental and demographic conditions of the feudal
community changed such that there appeared to be
overpopulation--more people than could be supported without
diminishing the seignioral share of the surplus
product--kings and lords often organized colonial invasion
(or resettlement) of other territories.

Like the advanced communal, deviations from population
homeostasis which might tend to produce overpopulation were
not infrequently met by net out-migration from the
established territory. This tended to extend the landed
estate and the military power of the lord or king though it
did not, inherently, alter the social relations of
production.

The corporate organization of feudal migration was an
important feature of medieval society. A second feature,
characteristic of feudal decline, was the scattering of
population caused by economic changes in rural areas which
forced peasants off the land. This represents the
emergence of what Marx was to call a "relative surplus
population" though it is not an essential component of
feudal society. The "surplus population" refers to a
sector of society which, for structural economic reasons,
is not fully employed but available for industrial work--or
potentially available in the case in which the surplus
population exists in non-industrial areas. These wandering
former serfs were eventually absorbed in the cities,
representing the form of migration known as "urbanization."

The Petty Comodity Mode of Production

Urbanization is also associated with petty commodity
production. The petty commodity mode is based upon

small-scale simple commodity production often taking place
in family units. Petty producers are mediated with one
another and with other economic actors by a merchant class.
This mode of production is least likely to dominate a
society (Amin, 1976: 13-14) for two reasons. On the one
hand, as a mode of production, the extraction of surplus
value is undertaken by a merchant class rather than by a
class which controls labor and owns the means of
production. On the other hand, the existence of a state
apparatus does not necessarily figure into the logic of the
petty commodity mode of production. Capital accumulation
by merchants is separated from the actual production of
commodities by the petty producers' exclusive control over
their own labor time. However, the acquisition of control
over petty producers' labor by the merchant class (by means
of its accumulated capital) presents fertile ground for the
growth of a capitalist economy. In this sense, the petty
commodity mode of production could be seen as an appendage
to any of the other pre-capitalist modes of production,
facilitating the transition to capitalism.

Amin's conception of this mode of production (his
"simple petty commodity mode of production") specifically
excludes agriculture. While it may be true that many of
the petty producers were separated from direct access to
the land, I see no theoretical reason for restricting its

useage. One might even argue that the imposition of cash cropping upon traditional African societies by the colonial powers in the capitalist epoch represents the attachment of the petty commodity mode of production to another pre-capitalist or even primitive communal mode.

Petty commodity production--whether of handicrafts or of agricultural goods--includes two dimensions of the division of labor. One dimension is within the production unit (especially the family, but also the master-apprentice shops) based upon personal characteristics like age, sex, or kinship. A second is based upon industry: the variety of guilds represented a non-class division of labor separating production by industry. The latent class-based division of labor rested in the master-apprentice relationship to be developed in the course of the accumulation process. Unlike feudal domains, advanced communal villages, and some configurations of slave society, the diversity of production available to society as a whole would not be reflected in the output of each petty commodity production unit. Again, the merchant class is essential to this mode of production in order to facilitate the acquisition of the means of consumption and to enter the commodities produced into circulation.

Because of the division of labor along lines of industry, production takes place most effectively in the

context of towns and cities with their access to
comprehensive markets. The form of migration most
associated with the petty commodity mode of production,
therefore, is urbanization. Migration, in this case,
serves to bring face-to-face with one another the two
essential classes of the petty commodity mode of
production.

Pre-Capitalist Differences Summarized

To summarize the argument thus far, the pre-capitalist
modes of production differ from the primitive communal in
that they represent the development of class society and
the state. While in most class societies several different
social classes may be found, the class formation which
defines the dominant mode of production is characterized by
the pre-eminence of two antagonistic classes. Migration is
one means by which this antagonism is resolved. In the
advanced communal mode of production, these classes are
represented by a dynastic ruling class vis-a-vis village
communes. Migration of entire communities, under state
authority, is one means by which the peasantry serves as
the force which expands the scope of power of the ruling
class. Individual migration to the outer reaches of the
territory, often to escape the oppression of the state, is
a means by which the state's territorial authority is

enlarged as the residents of newly-formed outlying communities are brought back into the realm of the kingdom. In the slave mode of production, forced migration of slaves (facilitated by the state) extends the power of the slave-owning class. And under feudalism, colonization serves to extend the geographical--if not always the economic--power of the feudal lords.

The advanced communal is distinguished from the other pre-capitalist modes of production particularly by direct state appropriation of surplus value through its class role in production. Slavery is characterized by the private appropriation of labor power by means of ownership of the actual persons of the producing classes. In this respect slavery differs from all others. In the petty commodity mode of production, labor power is neither privately appropriated as in feudalism or slavery, nor is labor power directly appropriated by the state as in the advanced communal. Surplus value is realized in the sphere of exchange. Feudalism is distinguished from the others in the sense that: serfdom is a private appropriation of labor power as opposed to state appropriation (in advanced communalism); serfs (unlike slaves) were systematically guaranteed some degree of control over their own labor and had legal status as persons; and, unlike the non-appropriation of labor power under the petty commodity mode of production, serf labor was partially appropriated by private interests.

A common feature of all pre-capitalist modes (perhaps excepting the petty commodity) is that migration is an important means by which tendencies toward overpopulation are corrected. The petty commodity mode probably establishes the broadest homeostatic limits (measured by population density) varying from isolated family farms to the clustering of workshops within urban areas. The wide range of possible population densities is probably due to the tendency of the petty commodity mode of production to be found attached to other modes of production. Petty production may represent socio-economic adaptation to an increasing population: a process by which homeostasis is increased through social structural change. None of the pre-capitalist modes of production require a relative surplus population though the feudal, at least, would seem under certain conditions to be responsible for the generation of one. A relative surplus population would be completely alien to a slave system--it would neither create not require one. These features, the relative surplus population and migration as a means of relieving possible overpopulation, help distinguish the pre-capitalist from the capitalist mode of production.

The Capitalist Epoch

The third major epoch experienced by human civilization is the capitalist. Unlike pre-capitalist and primitive communal modes of production, capitalism is marked by the accumulation of capital by means of the extraction of surplus value through the employment of wage labor in commodity production. According to Marx (1964: 67):

> One of the prerequisites of wage labor and one of the historic conditions for capital is free labour and the exchange of free labour against money, in order to reproduce money and convert it into values, in order to be consumed by money, not as use value for enjoyment, but as use value for money. Another prerequisite is the separation of free labour from the objective conditions of its realization--from the means and material of labour. This means above all that the worker must be separated from the land, which functions as his natural laboratory. This means the dissolution both of free petty land ownership and of communal landed property, . . .

The producing class under capitalism, then, is characterized by propertylessness and the release of bonds of servitude to the state, the slave master, and the feudal lord. Under capitalism the worker becomes a free agent, able to sell his or her labor time to whoever is willing to purchase it--and (within certain limits) make him or herself available wherever the demand for labor exists. Labor migration, therefore, is an essential feature of capitalism.

The corporate nature of migration which strengthened
pre-capitalist modes of production (except the petty
commodity), should be distinguished from the individual
nature of international labor migration in the capitalist
epoch. This is not to say that international labor
migration is lacking organization or corporate sanction.
Often the migration streams which have developed have been
encouraged by private or governmental interests in the
country of destination. This, however, differs markedly
from colonial and other types of pre-capitalist migration
in which organization and incentive were based in the
country of emigration and constituted a territorial
expansion. Despite this difference, distinct social
patterns in international migration in the capitalist epoch
remain.

The specific social patterns of migration in the
capitalist epoch differ according to the stage or phase of
capitalism and the specific characterisics of the countries
involved. These stages (and subdivisions within) are
variously defined; the most widely accepted being either
the Leninist (Lenin, 1970) division of capitalism into the
industrial and imperialist stages or Baran and Sweezy's
(1966) division into competitive and monopoly capital.
Mandel (1978) has suggested that a period of "late
capitalism" has now evolved.

The competitive capital period was characterized by relatively free access to markets and by numerous small companies in competition with one another. This period is distinguished from the monopoly capital period which followed, the latter characterized by the growth and consolidation of control of markets and production in the hands of a small number of companies. What must also be examined in the analysis of international migration is the economic incongruity among nations.

Structural Discord and Economic Development

When more than one mode of production should appear in a system, whether we speak of a national or transnational system, the possibility of structural discord must be addressed. For example, the petty commodity mode of production, as I shall point out in a subsequent chapter, coexisted within the generally feudal society of late medieval England. While this relationship eventually contributed to the downfall of English feudalism, it also contributed to the rise of capitalism and the success of the British economy in the Industrial Revolution. In some situations, however, structurally incompatible modes of production appear within a given system causing stagnation and preventing its further development.[18] Historically,

---

[18] I have addressed this in the context of capitalist

the structurally discordant combination of modes of
production which cause systemic stagnation have usually
appeared within the context of single nations. The
harmoneous combination of modes of production may appear
either within a single nation or a transnational system.
Perhaps the best example of this is the modern imperialist
system which has contributed toward previously unthinkable
degrees of economic growth. Of course, this growth has
taken place unevenly with those nations possessing the more
fully advanced capitalist economies the main beneficiaries.
The underdeveloped countries have generally undergone
periods of great adversity. The underdeveloped countries,
I am suggesting, do not suffer the adverse effects of
structural discord at the transnational level, but at the
national level as their pre-capitalist modes of production
have had certain elements of the social relations of
capitalism (distribution and exchange) superimposed upon
society such that complete dissolution of the
pre-capitalist productive forces is prevented.

   With regard to migration, the pattern of structual
discord has important implications. When a mode of
production dissolves from forces at work within the society
in question, as I shall argue was the English case, the

_____

underdevelopment and disharmoney within the spheres of
production in Elliott (1978: 147).

tendency is for a structurally harmonious (if politically disruptive) development to take place. The dissolution of English feudalism and the growth of English capitalism, mediated by petty commodity production, was one of the most important features of the great redistribution of population from the rural areas to the cities. This type of migration, though accompanied by conflict and misery for the generations of population displaced, served to provide one of the prerequisites by which Britain entered into the capitalist epoch.

In modern underdeveloped countries, the imposition of capitalist techiques and organization of production in rural areas with inadequate provision for industrialization in these countries represents a structural discord within the nation: for example, the capitalist mode of production in agriculture, petty commodity mode in industry. In such a case, the tendency is for emigration as the structural changes have effectively lowered national population homeostasis. Social changes in such countries have often introduced improvements in health which have the tendency of lowering the death rate, thus pushing the actual size of the population still upward. Decreased fertility often does not correct the tendency toward overpopulation, caused by economic and medical changes, because the economic changes themselves have been contradictory. While the need for rural labor has decreased and the need for urban labor has not increased commensurately, the social welfare of the aged rural population has not improved sufficiently to counter the need for a large, extended family to support the dependent population. The availability of modern banking systems, however, has meant that the dependent members of the family could be supported by emigrant workers whose remittances help sustain the family, and in some cases entire communities. Such remittances may provide sufficient investment capital to actually initiate industrial production and contribute to the dissolution of the discordant structures and the development of capitalism.

In the nineteenth century, England had virtually exhausted its relative surplus population by the relatively full absorption of the displaced rural population into the industrial sector. There was, however, noticable immigration into England of Irish, Welsh, Scottish, and other workers to make up for the depleted English "reserve army". Once a capitalist country had so absorbed its displaced rural population, without substantial immigration, it would tend to face a crisis period. The potential crisis would result from the rising strength of labor (due to the depletion of a major section of the relative surplus population) which tends to erode

capitalist profits and the ability of the capitalist class
to accumulate, thus throwing into disarray the capitalist
economy, itself. Such a crisis has been largely avoided
thus far in the capitalist epoch by the export of capital
from such countries and the availability of immigrants from
elsewhere in the world system, workers made redundant and
unemployable by structural discord within their own
countries. United States history represents a particular
variant of this development.

In the nineteenth century, the United States was
effectively divided into a structurally discordant nation.
The caste system of the American South, both during the
period of slavery and for a number of post-bellum
generations, effectively blocked the release of black
agricultural workers and the development of a modern rural
economy. The Northeast, however, had begun its transition
to capitalism in large part by the immigration of petty
commodity producers in the seventeenth and eighteenth
centuries, followed by workers from of England, Germany,
and other countries. The importation of investment capital
from Europe also helped fuel American capitalist industry
in the nineteenth century. In order to fill the need for
unskilled labor which could not be fully provided by the
southern system or the relatively modest eastern and
western agricultural workers, vast numbers of European

immigrants departed nations in which the industrial sector
did not grow rapidly enough to absorb them.

The North-South structural discord within the U.S.
(the existence of southern sharecropping which failed to
free laborers vis-a-vis northern industrial development
which required massive labor inputs) was eventually
resolved in part by dissolution of sharecropping and the
great migration of southern blacks to the northern cities.
At the same time, the world system was changing such that
the colonized countries of Asia and Latin America, in
particular, had developed their own periods of structural
discord and capitalist underdevelopment.

I see capitalist underdevelopment as a specific kind
of structural discord. It is unlike the English model of
feudalism and petty commodity production or the American
model of slavery and industrial capitalism. With regard to
underdevelopment, the modes of production (capitalist and a
pre-capitalist) are articulated in such a way that certain
features of the capitalist relations of production act to
constrain the development of the productive forces by the
way the spheres of exchange and distribution join the
society with the international system.

The following chapter addresses problems of
methodology. In it I discuss the sources of data and
information, how these were obtained, and how they are

analysed. At the end of the chapter I propose eleven
working hypotheses which are more fully addressed at the
appropriate places in the body of the thesis. These are
not intended to be formal, operationalized hypotheses
suitable for testing. The working hypotheses are, rather,
possible explanations for historical phenomena which are
derived from the homeostatic model.

CHAPTER IV

METHODOLOGY

Having reviewed the main theoretical currents underlying this thesis it remains to elaborate the means by which it will be explored. Therefore, the present chapter, on the means by which the more theoretical and abstract thesis is to be joined with the more concrete analysis, discusses the methods utilized to effect such a joining.

Historical Sociology

Historical sociology, as I see it, is neither a substantive area such as sociology of the family or industrial sociology nor is it a method in the sense of, for example, "qualitative" or "quantitative" methods. Historical sociology is, according to Abrams[19] (1982: xv), a problematic of structure:

> I would almost say that it is a question of trying to build a sociology of process as an alternative to our tried, worn and inadequate sociologies of action and system. And that is where the problematic of structuring comes in.

---

[19] I find Abrams' conception of historical sociology particularly illuminating and a model worthy of careful consideration.

> It re-unites sociology with the other human
> sciences, especially history. And it does so,
> not by way of a casual marriage of defective
> theory to an unprincipled empiricism, but through
> the re-discovery of an authentic and fundamental
> common interest.

Historical sociology, as I have tried to write it, superimposes a theoretical structure over the actual human process of population movement and redstribution within the larger process of societal development. The subject matter of historical sociology, and the historical sources, are derived from surviving (usually written) remnants of the actual human process.

The present chapter addresses the means by which the subject matter is extracted from the human process and structured within the problematic. It serves to alert the reader to the sources and methods by which the thesis was developed, merged into the problematic, and ultimately expressed within the substance of the study, which appears in chapters five through eleven.

Data and Sources

The bulk of this study is based on secondary sources. In addition to conventional secondary sources, I have gained access to various empirical data collected by numerous independent researchers. Government data were also utilized where available.

Most economic time series reproduced graphically in
chapter eight are from Bowden (1967), the statistical
appendix to volume IV of The Agrarian History of England
and Wales. The disaggregated price indices are from Brown
and Hopkins (1981). The population figures in chapter
eight are from Wrigley (1969), Chandler and Fox (1974),
Tilly (1975), and Clarkson (1971). The migration data
utilized in the time series analyses of chapters ten and
eleven are taken from Bromwell (1969) and Immigration
Commission (1911b). All other data utilized in the time
series analysis are from Inter-University Consortium for
Political and Social Research (ICPSR) tape number 7412
"Cross-National Time Series: 1815-1973" (1976) collected
by Arthur Banks.

Historical Sources and Methods

My selection of secondary sources consisted of a
filtering process in which the various kinds of raw
material which I believed pertinent, from contemporary
narratives to state documents to geographical
evidence--almost all of which was inaccessible to me
directly--was approached through the writings of those
scholars who had mastered the various methods and
techniques necessary to dislodge and disseminate this
material to those lacking direct access. A summary of such

methods through which I (indirectly) gained access to the raw material of the historical process follows.

Social History

Most conventional history writing is little more than a narrative or chronicle of the exploits of the ruling class. What the ruling class did, of course, cannot be ignored. In recent generations, however, a school of history has emerged which considers the common people of historical societies worthy of examination. Many such historians have been influenced by the ideas of Marx and Engels, particularly the idea that social history is the history of class struggles.

This orientation has led historians to enquire into the conditions facing the peoples who performed the labor of producing and reproducing society's subsistence. Among historians of English society, E.P. Thompson (1966) stands out as the archetypical example of social historians. The social historian is to history much what the ethnographer is to sociology. Rodney Hilton's (1973) study of the 1381 English peasant revolt is a good example. Another example is Raftis (1964) who has carefully examined extant records in the Ramsey villages of England to reconstruct the patterns of migration in the feudal period. Such studies, which trace the movement of individuals and families by the parish records, lend considerable insight into lifestyle and mobility in past ages.

Economic History

Perhaps a more established tradition within history is economic history. This field, which blends with social history in many studies (e.g. Gregg, 1976; Williams, 1966), is often more quantitative and more oriented toward population aggregates and trends than social history. Indeed, G.D.H. Cole (1954) begins and ends his text with population data.

While a few bold authors have attempted to draw the outlines of a grand economic history of the world (e.g. Caldwell, 1978; Cipolla, 1978) with population and environment playing important roles in their schemes, most economic historians have restricted their inquiries to single countries and single historical periods (e.g. Ashton, 1955) or even more narrowly to specific topics. Of the latter, the researches of Brown and Hopkins (1981) and Lord Beveridge (1939) into English wages and prices through the centuries lend an important temporal dimension to analyses of economic life. This helps to bring into comparative perspective the historically diverse studies of the social historians. Many economic historians have provided important data which sociologists and demographers

are wont to make use of in time series analyses. I shall
have more to say about time series analysis shortly.

Historical Geography

Historians in general, and all students of past
civiliations, make use of the written record as available.
In some cases, however, little or no written record
remains. Historical geography has developed a general
method by which various evidence of past settlements may
yield important information about the migrations of peoples
of the distant past. With regard to Western Europe, East
(1967: 118-122) has outlined the major sources of the raw
material of historical geographers. In addition to
traditional written historical evidence accessible to, and
utilized by historians, geographers have found the analysis
of place names an important source of information about
migrations of ethnic and tribal groups. Such analysis
requires training in linguistics and has revealed, for
example, the extent of Danish settlement in England in the
early middle ages.

Archeology also plays a role in the historical
geographer's inquiry into migration and settlement. But
where the historical geographical method makes its primary
contribution is in site interpretation--a survey of modern
geographical conditions. By on-site surveys and air

mapping, the locations of ruins of buildings and entire villages may be found. In addition, the centuries-old patterns of field perimeters and even plow marks may be discerned. Such data lend important insights into both forces and relations of production at specific locations where there may be a dearth of surviving written records. Such evidence has been assembled by Beresford (1954) to locate sites of medieval English village depopulations.

Historical Demography

Hisorical deomgraphy is less a subdivision of an established discipline, such as history, sociology, or geography, as it is an interdisciplinary method. Historical demographers attempt the statistical reconstruction of trends in past populations. Births, deaths, marriages, movements, etc. are all subject to historical analysis on the basis of documents which record vital statistics and census enumerations. Many of the data developed by historical demographers are estimates, often made on the basis of fragmentary records and generalized to a larger or different population, or interpolated between records available for different time periods. Precise estimates of migration prior to the nineteenth century are among the most difficult to develop.

One means of estimating population movement consists of census analysis. Louis Schade (1856) was among the first to utilize a relatively modern technique for estimating United States immigration on the basis of the decennial censuses. In a political pamphlet supporting unrestricted immigration, Schade attempted to calculate the yearly immigration from 1790 to 1850 on the basis of the difference between the population enumerated at each census and the expected enumeration had there been no immigration. Such analyses utilize known or estimated birth and death rates. Another technique used by Ravenstein (1885; 1889) was the analysis of the places of birth found in census returns.

The previous paragraphs have outlined the main historical methods by which I have indirectly gained access to qualitative and quantitative historical data and have benefitted from previous interpretations and analyses of these data. The statistical method I used is discussed next.

Statistical Method: Time Series Analysis

The empirical data are in the form of time series and I have utilized a statistical technique from within the assortment of time series analysis methods. Time series analysis, in its most general application, is the analysis of changes in empirical data over time, in Uslaner's (1978: 7) words, "Anything that moves!" There are various techniques of time series analysis, each possessing certain prerequisites to which the data must conform. One of the most general such prerequisite is that the data must be discrete and compiled at periodic intervals. To borrow an example from the physical sciences, changes in temperature could not be analysed as a time series in the <u>continuous</u> series in which temperature change actually takes place, but only on the basis of a sampling of temperatures at regularly recuring periods: minutes, hours, days, etc.

Once the discrete and periodic nature of the data has been established, the actual analysis would proceed on the basis of the goal or purpose of the analysis. One of the traditional and most fundamental interests of social scientists conducting time series analysis is to discern any regularly recurring patterns or cycles in the series. The two techniques most often used are the moving average and the fitting of a trend or curve to the original series.

The conventional moving average model smooths the peaks and troughs of a time series by averaging a specified number (e.g. nine for a nine-year moving average) of original data values and replacing (normally) the central datum with this average. The process is repeated for each data value in turn. This not only reduces the amplitude of the peaks and troughs but it also reduces the effect of cycles of less than twice the moving average. As a method, per se, it is relatively inelegant and useful mainly for the purpose of displaying graphically a smoothed version of an original series. Much more sophisticated techniques, however, derive from the basic moving average calculation.

Curve fitting techniques vary. The simplest and most crude technique consists of the visual fitting of a line intended to represent the trend of a series over time. A somewhat more sophisticated model, but one which still depends upon the judgement of the analyist on the basis of a visual examination of the series, is the fitting of algebraic or exponential functions to data. More sophisticated still, is the fitting of a least squares polynomial curve of predetermined degree. For example, if the raw data suggest a parabolic trend, a second degree polynomial would be fitted to the original so as to minimize the sum of squares of difference between the original series and the constructed polynomial trend line.

One of the fundamental assumptions of a time series analysis is that the time order of observations is an important component of the model. For example, in most cross sectional analyses, the ordering of observations is relatively arbitrary and plays no role in the calculation of statistics of correlation, etc. In such multivariate analyses, correlation is based upon the relationships among variables such that changes in the dependent variable are predicted on the basis of changes in the independents. In the typical time series analysis, however, the most recent values of the dependent variable are thought to be the best predictors of the current value. This phenomenon is called autocorrelation.

In the present analysis, the effects of autocorrelation tended to bias the results of my multiple regression analysis. I faced this problem because my goal was to determine the multivariate relationships among certain economic and demographic time series, not to forecast future values (where the autocorrelation phenomenon is used).

In chapters ten and eleven, analysis of the correlation between migration and economic variables suggested by the Thomas (1973) findings (and others believed theoretically important), consisted of a succession of two-step full transformations of regression equations in order to extract from among the independent variables those which remained significant, discarding those which failed to attain t-ratios of at least 2.00. The two-step transformation method is a means of detrending and removing the effects of autocorrelation from time series models. The two-step transformation was performed

by the SAS Autoreg program (SAS, 1982: 187-202) on the IBM
4341 computer.

Units of Analysis

In the application of the homeostatic hypothesis to a
qualitative analysis, the unit of analysis would be a
geo-political unit. As different units of analysis may
suggest qualitatively different relationships among
variables, just what specific unit is most appropriate
depends upon the questions to be pursued. Since I am
addressing migration, I shall define the units of analysis
according to the role migration plays within the
homeostatic model.

The smallest unit of analysis is the community. This
is also supposed to be the most homeogeneous unit such that
any patterns of population redistribution within the
community would not, in and of themsleves, be expected to
alter the population size. The community population would
only be expected to change, in the context of migration, by
net migration into or out of the community.

The middle unit of analysis is the nation. In the
context of the nation, population size depends not only
upon net migration into or out of the nation (as in the
community), but also upon redistribution within the nation.
Such redistribution usually suggests either the

colonization of unpopulated or "underpopulated" territories or the net movement of population between communities characterized by different levels of population homeostasis. The paramount example is urbanization, the movement of population from relatively low homeostatic rural communities to the cities characterized by high population homeostasis. This is one example of intra-national migration which impacts upon national population size.

Another example concerns the national impact of local deviations from homeostasis. National population size will change in response not only to whatever localized event altered a component community's population, but also to the general tendency of other communities to change their basic population parameters to compensate for their roles in inter-community migration. Migration may greatly accelerate adaptation to the new conditions (by, for example, rapidly replacing population lost to natural disaster) and even, perhaps, contribute to national over-compensaton for the localized change as fertility increases in areas of net out-migration. Another effect may also be involved. When population redistribution involves removal from places with relatively high rates of natural increase (e.g. rural areas) to places of relatively low rates of natural increase (e.g. medieval cities), the impact of the migration may be to constrain population growth. By shifting a greater proportion of the population to areas with higher death rates or lower fertility rates, national population growth may be stopped or even reversed.

The world level is the final qualitative unit of analysis. In that, migration which affects population size takes place only within the world system, itself. It is constituted by both urbanization and international migration. Of course, there are intermediate levels: regions within a nation; international regions within the global system. Such intermediate units may assume the migration characteristics of the nation as a unit, though if empirical conditions seem to fit, they may be analysed on the basis of either the community or the world unit of analysis. There is likely to be some error involved, but the simplification of the analysis may yield rewards which warrant the error factor. At a later point in the present study, I utilize the "Atlantic economy" as a world-level unit, focusing upon certain trans-Atlantic migration streams.

Hypotheses

One of the major points of analysis underlying this study is the hypothesis that migration is one possible demographic result of systemic changes introduced by either the social structure or the environment into the general system of population homeostasis. There are other means of correcting departures from homeostasis, such as changes in fertility or mortality, but migration is seen as the one which effects the greatest social impact, itself, upon the social system by changes in the age or sex composition of the population or the introduction of alien cultures, ideologies, technologies, etc. The following hypotheses are designed to help explain certian historical processes related to migration on the basis of the structural thesis elaborated in the problematic. The hypotheses themselves represent the articulation of the problematic within specific historical contexts.

Hypothesis One

The dominant type of peasant subjugation under feudalism (to lord or to land) determines the primary type of corporate migration (conquest or colonial settlement).

The first hypothesis is that the structural relation between medieval corporate migration and the

feudal social structure is best explained on the basis of
the two-fold nature of peasant subjugation: European serfs
were bound both to lord and land. While the particulars of
this bondage varied in different countries and in different
periods, the specific relationship operative at any given
time influenced the type of corporate migration which took
place: dominance of the political bond between lord and
serf encouraged conquest migration in which one nation
would conquer another; and dominance of the economic bond
of serf to land (mediated by the political bond) resulted
in colonial settlement migration in which waste land was
brought under cultivation by serfs in service to a lord.

Hypothesis Two

Colonial resettlement before the fourteenth century
population crisis established a pattern of population
distribution which could not withstand, within homeostatic
limits, the population retrogression.

My hypothesis is that the previous forms of
corporate migration, the settlement movement in particular,
established population size near the upper limits of the
homeostatic carrying capacity. This could not be
maintained in the face of the population crisis. I argue
that migration subsequent to the fourteenth century crisis
period did not, in itself, contribute to the downfall of

feudalism. It was the period of migration before the crisis which helped prepare the demographic deathbed of feudalism.

Hypothesis Three

Socio-economic reprganization after the fourteenth century population crisis established a lower population homeostasis.

In chapter six, a structural change in class formation and in the class dimension of state intervention into peasant affairs is hypothesized as having taken place in the context of a socio-economic reorganization which effected the establishment of population homeostasis at a lower, post-crisis level.

Hypothesis Four

Cultural practices maintained population homeostasis at the lower, post-crisis level.

With regard to population stagnation, I suggest that the primary demographic means by which the social structure maintained the lower post-crisis level of population homeostasis was through cultural practices. Specifically, an increase in the normative age of marriage and in changes household composition patterns--increased presence of nuclear as opposed to extended families--helped to constrain the regrowth of population and also contributed to the general mobility of the population.

Hypothesis Five

Overseas colonial emigration and rural depopulation contributed to the sixteenth century price revolution.

In the analysis of the economic antecedents of the seventeenth century crisis in chapter eight, most particularly the sixteenth century price revolution, my hypothesis is that population factors were associated with the inflation in two major ways. On the one hand, the net out-migration from the European system in the early colonial period was countered economically by a net importation of specie. This increase in the total quantity of gold and silver in Europe, I would argue, contributed to the price revolution.[20] On the other hand, demand-pull inflation which originated in the agricultural sector of late feudal society was itself the result of the regrowth of the rural population, once the period of population stagnation had passed.

---

[20] I am working here with the European system as the unit of analysis. I am not suggesting an exact country-by-country correspondence between flows of specie and persons.

Hypothesis Six

Environmental factors in the post-crisis period constrained
the actual population size to the lower limits of
population homeostasis.

Regarding mortality and the demographic
transition discussed in chapter eight, my hypothesis is
that two major environmental factors acted to keep
population near the lower limits of the homeostatic
carrying capacity. Periodic episodes of high mortality due
to pestilence and crop failures acted to constrain
population far below its theoretical carrying capacity.
This is to be distinguished from the establishment of a
lower population homeostasis, per se. Countering this
tendency, however, were environmental and socio-economic
changes which acted to establish a higher population
homeostasis. (The ultimate relief from
environmentally-caused mortality allowed the size of the
population to rise toward its optimum level.)

Hypothesis Seven

From the time of the price revolution, socio-economic
changes contributed to a higher population homeostasis.

A further dimension of the foregoing is the
hypothesis that in the course of the socio-economic

adaptation to the environmental pressure on population, a situation presenting the potential for increase in the actual population size could be said to exist, awaiting diminution especially of the urban mortality rate. Demographically, this adaptation appeared in the form of high rural fertility coupled with high rates of urbanization (population redistribution from areas of relatively high rates of natural increase to to areas of relatively low natural increase. In addition, consumption patterns may have been altered. There are important class implications of this socio-economic adaptation which help explain questions of class formation discussed in previous chapters. Changes associated with consumption likely contributed to the restructuring of the urban economy so as to establish the petty commodity mode of production, and most importantly, the class base upon which it rested: a prosperous merchant class and a skilled class of artisan petty producers. The increased agricultural production for market suggests a parallel class development in rural areas.

Hypothesis Eight

Environmentally and economically induced mortality declines initiated actual population growth.

Concomitant with the eventual passing of the
plague (for environmental reasons which are not fully
understood), came the economic ability and technical
feasibility for merchants and municipalities to store and
transport sufficient quantities of grain to relieve the
potential of famine, especially in the cities. Population
and economic growth so induced, alongside dissolution of
rural feudalism and other social changes, are hypothesized
as having provided both the ready workforce and the capital
necessary for the onset of industrial capitalist
production.

Hypothesis Nine

Coerced migration was a precondition for the development of
industrial capitalism in North America.

The central hypothesis of chapter nine is that
coerced migration of laborers to the Americas—if not
slavery, per se—was a necessary condition for the
emergence of the Atlantic economy as it appeared on the eve
of the industrial capitalist epoch. The structural discord
within the European economy, especially Britain vis-a-vis
Iberia, dictated the differential patterns of forced labor
and trans-Atlantic migration which appeared in the
sixteenth through the eighteenth centuries. The loci of
slavery and indentured servitude in the Americas helped

determine the most viable sites for the development of
capitalism there.

The wage labor upon which capitalism rested emerged
first where free immigrants and indentured workers (unlike
slaves) could enter the open labor market. Capitalist
development proceeded on far less firm footing in areas
where slavery persisted due to the inability of most slaves
to enter into the free wage labor market. Even when
slavery had been abolished, the racial-caste system
required under the slave mode of production as it appeared
in much of the Americas continued to operate, further
smothering the potential for a free work force of wage
laborers bound to neither land nor master. The possibility
of wage labor developing in areas where non-class societies
persisted was even slighter, still. In summary, capitalism
developed first where labor had been imported and was most
readily freed to enter the wage labor work force.

Hypothesis Ten

The conditions of industrial economies constitute important
influences on international migration.

With regard to free trans-Atlantic migration in
the industrial capitalist epoch, hypothesis ten
specifically concerns migration of industrial workers.
Among industrialized (or industrializing) countries the

state of the national economy of the country of emigration would exercise an important influence upon the patterns of migration to the U.S.

Hypothesis Eleven

Changes in rural population size are directly related to changes in emigration.

In the late feudal, early industrial countries of Europe, migration to the U.S. would be directly influenced at least in part by changes in the size of the rural population (reflecting changes in Marx's "latent reserve army.") Migration was also subject to environmental interventions, especially inclement weather, which tended to impact migration series with sudden shocks.

Hypothesis Twelve

During the transition from industrial capitalism to imperialism, economic factors demonstrate greater influence on international migration than do non-economic factors.

Hypothesis twelve derives from a variant of Marxian theory, often associated with Lenin, which suggests that the 1870s saw a major turning point in capitalist development. In the early "industrial" stage, capital accumulation was derived mainly from the export of commodities by the most advanced capitalist countries. In the later "imperialist" stage, capital accumulation was derived from the export of capital for investment abroad. If this is correct, we should be able to discern a corresponding pattern of international labor migration. In a multivariate analysis, economic variables would be expected to become dominant over non-economic variables.

Since England is generally understood to have been the primary imperialist country at the conjuncture in question, I would expect that economic variables for other countries could assume greater importance in the imperialist stage than in the industrial stage of capitalism. This should be true whether we speak of net labor importing countries such as the United States (in which case an "economic pull" would be evident) or in net labor exporting countries. For the latter, at minimum, a diminishing of any evidence of "population push" would be expected. In addition, there should be seen a shift to economic pull factors where they were not previously evident.

CHAPTER V

THE FOURTEENTH CENTURY POPULATION CRISIS

Introduction

The present chapter surveys specific aspects of each
of the three elements of the homeostatic model--population,
environment, and social structure--at the historic turning
point of the European feudal mode of production, the
fourteenth century population crisis. I refer to this
period as a turning point in the sense that the hidden
socio-economic processes and the presumed gradual climatic
changes which had been underway for generations had allowed
a growth of population which, when assaulted by episodes of
environmental degradation, broached the ability of the
feudal social structure to maintain itself without
fundamental changes. In terms of the homeostatic model, we
could say that a combination of socio-economic factors
(through migration) and environmental factors (evidently a
fair climate) converged to drive the population to the
upper limits of the homeostatic carrying capacity.

With the intervention of adverse environmental conditions, most notably the 'Black Death," a series of bubonic plague epidemics which greatly increased mortality, class struggles and economic imperatives forced certain changes in the social structure which established a new and lower level of homeostasis. We have no detailed and little reliable knowledge of long-term climatic changes, nor of long-term trends in infectious disease in the early middle ages. However, we know that climate does change somewhat over the long term and that disease-causing agents are subject to evolutionary changes which increase or decrease the virulence of the agent. If we assume that climate or disease or some combination changed sufficiently in the centuries preceding the fourteenth, and there is some evidence to support this assumption (see Wallerstein, 1974: 37), a more favorable climate, for instance, could have given rise to a general tendency of local populations to increase.

Corporate Migration and Serf Labor in the Early Middle Ages

In a manuscript evidently not intended for publication, Marx (1964: 67) noted that "free labour" was one of the "historic conditions for capital". Free labor is bound neither to lord nor land and the laborers are therefore "free" to seek employment wherever and with whomever will have them. The importance of this insight into mobility and capitalism should become abundantly clear as this thesis unfolds. At this point, however, it provides an important clue in the search for the relationship between migration and the feudal social structure. The relationship suggests a more elaborate role for migration than is usually acknowledged in the dissolution of feudal society and the beginning of capitalism.

Let me first address migration and the feudal social structure in the period preceding the fourteenth century population crisis. The two major types of corporate migration--waste land settlement and conquering invasions--are discussed in the context of the Scandanavian invasions, the German movement onto Eastern Europe, and the colonization of waste lands in Britain. These are hypothesized as being related to the two-fold nature of peasant subjugation characteristic of feudalism--a bondage to both lord and land.

Hypothesis One

The dominant type of peasant subjugation under feudalism (to lord or to land) determines the primary type of corporate migration (conquest or colonial settlement).

Discussion

The structural relation between medieval corporate
migration and feudalism is best explained on the basis of
the two-fold nature of peasant subjugation. European serfs
were bound to both lord and land. While the particulars of
this bondage varied in different countries and in different
time periods, the specific relationship operative at any
given time influenced the type of corporate migration which
took place: dominance of the political bond between lord
and serf encouraged conquest migration in which one nation
would conquer another; dominance of the economic bond of
serf to land (mediated by the political bond) resulted in
colonial settlement migration in which additional land
would be brought under cultivation by serfs in service to a
lord.

The chief characteristic of the European fuedal system
was the lord-serf relationship. While the precise terms of
class relations between nobility and peasantry varied
through different parts of Europe, and over time, it can
clearly be said that the serfs were unfree. Particularly
in the early middle ages, the lord-serf relationship was
primarily political, manifested in elaborate systems of
homage. Accordingly, the peasants' surplus product could
be said to have been "transferred under coercive sanction",

though historically (9th and 10th centuries), some quid pro
quo with the lords providing some protection may have been
involved (Hilton, 1949: 118). One consequence of the
political relationship was that the pre-feudal allodial
(peasant-owned landed) property was gradually converted
into manorial property with the peasants remaining on as
tenant serfs (Hilton, 1973: 42-43). The emergence of
tenancy may have prompted scholars to conceptualize as rent
the surplus value appropriated by the nobility. In so
conceptualizing the surplus extracted from the peasantry as
rent, Hilton (1949: 119-121) nevertheless recognizes that
the serf was bound to both the lord and the land, at least
as of the fourteenth century. Moreover, Bloch (1961:
248ff) notes that it was the "custom of the manor" which
regulated the lord-serf relations, a situation which may
have obscured the two-fold (rent/homage) nature of peasant
exploitation.

The dualistic nature of peasant subjugation, at least
through the thirteenth century, established the basic
parameters of peasant mobility or migration. Two types of
peasant corporate migration took place in the early middle
ages (or Bloch's "first feudal age"): conquest migration
and waste land settlement. Let me examine each in turn.

History has recorded numerous examples of invasion and
conquest, not the least of which took place in Europe and

have continued to do so even into the present century.
C.T. Smith (1967: 154-55) cites the Scandinavian invasions
of the 9th and 10th centuries, the "looting, raiding, and
burning," as having contributed toward the military aspects
of feudal organiztion and the need for walled medieval
towns. For example, the Scandinavian invaders did not
permanently establish themselves in Ireland (which was not
feudalized until the Tudor conquest) though some did
permanently emigrate to Normandy and England (Jackson,
1973: 33-34; 44) which were defended by, and production
organized around feudal practices.[21] Military
organization, no doubt, reinforced the traditional practice
of homage and vassalage in feudal Europe--a hierarchial
relationship which ran throughout the fabric of feudal
society--though the material rewards received by the
nobility from the peasantry through this system may well
have been more important in its perpetuation than were its
ability to defend against unwanted immigration. At any
rate, neither tenancy nor social hierarchy seem to have
suffered--and the hierarchial system may well have been
strengthened--in the face of the Scandinavian conquest and
immigration.

-----

[21] Place name evidence and the eleventh century
Domesday Book indicate that there may have been a very
substantial and lasting Danish presence in the north and
east of England, though there is no consensus on this
point (Darby, 1973: 1-38).

The Scandinavian episodes, which did not result in substantial settlement of land, represented the bondage of serf to lord rather than of serf to land.

Another example of conquest and migration in the early middle ages (a movement which was to persist intermittantly in one form or another well into the 20th century) was the German advance and permanent settlement east and into the Balkins. German settlers followed the frontier trade established by military conquests of Slavs and Avars while Dutch and Flemish immigrants were brought in as colonists (East, 1966: 75, 81-83). While the military aspects of German expansion (and especially Scandinavian invasions) may have overshadowed the clearing and settlement of sparsely populated regions, this latter development occurred throughout feudal Europe--under church and seignorial direction, if not directly by military conquest.

The German invasions also represent the power of the lord-serf bond. But the resulting settlement, and perhaps more important than settlement alone, the change in the mode of production which dominated the Balkins, demonstrates the feudal bondage to the land as a systemic phenomenon. This combination of military and settler migration demonstrates an important linkage between the social structure and population movement in the feudal epoch.

It was this "Age of Clearing" which exposed the interconnections among peasant agriculture, political subjugation, and migration. This period, lasting from about 1050 to 1300 especially in Britain, France, and Germany, was characterized by rapid population growth and the major extension of cultivation into forest, marsh, and other "waste lands." While the clearing of waste lands was known to accompany both the Scandinavian and German conquests (Darby, 1973: 1-38; East, 1966: 82), the role of migration and settlement in the early middle ages is best revealed in such areas as Britain and France where the local ruling classes, the secular and cleric landlords, sought to enforce the extension of cultivation into hitherto uncultivated areas within close enough proximity to their estates that they could maintain, if not increase, the level of surplus product extracted from the peasantry under conditions of population growth. The settlement movements outside Germany, particularly in Britain and France, probably represented the dominance of the serf-land bond over the lord-serf bond. It is true that these migrations were largely directed by the gentry, but--this is important--the extension of cultivation for the purpose of maintaining the existing feudal system seems to have been the primary motive force.

The specific incentives for the ruling class (clergy and lay lords) to encourage "more intensive use of the waste lands they had in their control" (Smith, 1967: 166) were: for the church, an increase in the tithe; for all landlords, an increase in rents; and for the state, an increase in proceeds from dispensing justice, taxes on an increasing population, and greater military power. At this historical distance, it is probably impossible to sort out the relative contributions of settlement and the population growth rate in providing the ruling class with a greater surplus to extract, but it is likely that neither population growth itself nor the expansion of cultivation alone could have made as great a contribution without the other. In fact, it could be argued that either one acting alone would have tended to decrease the total surplus transferred from the peasantry to the nobility.

In terms of the homeostatic model, I would argue (assuming no change in technology) that population growth without the expansion of cultivation would tend to erode the economic foundation of the feudal ruling class in at least two possible ways. For one, the absolute quantity of surplus product would tend to diminish as more was required to feed the greater population. Secondly, there would likely be an additional tendency, regardless of the extent to which the first was operative, toward the diminishing of the individual peasant share of the produce. This could, under certain conditions, encourage revolt and class struggles against the feudal rulers. However, the essentially conservative peasantry--seldom willing to question established authority--was motivated to accede to the nobility's demands to extend the spatial dimensions of cultivation. On the one hand, in the face of population growth without a fundamental change in the social relations of production, more land was likely to have been required to maintain the subsistance level and still generate the surplus required by the ruling class. On the other hand, the ruling class offered incentives to the serfs to open waste lands to cultivation: lower rents, dues, and labor services; lighter fines; and more personal freedom.

By the beginning of the fourteenth century, English feudal society--coexisting alongside the medieval towns which shall be discussed subsequently--consisted of (1) a monarchial ruling class of nobility and clergy; and (2) a growing peasantry, many (if not most) of whom were subjects of lay or ecclesiastical landlords. While the peasantry was a conservative one with strong attachments to tradition and church, the middle ages saw considerable conflict, not all of which was chivalrous, intra-ruling class struggles for dominance and power. Class struggle between the enserfed peasantry and the feudal nobility took place as well. Hilton's (1948; 1973) research reveals that at least as early as the thirteenth century, England saw peasant resistance to the seignorial class. Peasant resistance was rooted to a large extent in their lords' intensified exploitation through increased rent and labor services, particularly where migration was not institutionalized because recourse to the colonization or settlement of waste lands was not available. In most cases, however, the economic pressures of the early middle ages, where they were increased, were resolved by expanded cultivation.

In summary, if one accepts the evidence of population growth, migration could be said to serve as a means of maintaining the political status quo until the end of the early middle ages (c.1300). There were few changes in the social relations of production, though some apparent reduction of oppression was allowed in the maintenance of the feudal system.

Political Economy of the Crisis

Fourteenth century events mark the era as a convenient dividing point between the early and later middle ages. This conjuncture saw significant changes in the medieval population--changes which contributed to the ongoing dissolution of European feudal society.

There is no way to know all the reasons for the population growth in the last few centuries of the early middle ages. Colonization, a result of population increase, may itself have contributed to further population increase in the colonized areas. Donkin (1973: 76-77) argues that increased fertility due to a lowering in the age of marriage,[22] may have appeared in colonized areas. It seems likely that environmental factors, particularly a more favorable climate, contributed to the population increase. The drastic drop in population, much of which took place in the fourteenth century, is linked to high mortality. It was this sudden population decline and subsequent peasant migrations which, under conditions I shall elaborate below, hastened the collapse of feudal society.

According to Helliener (1967: 68), "The great European famine of 1315-17 may have been the first harbinger of disaster." Subsequently, the "Black Death" (the plagues of 1349, the 1360s, the 1370s) and the Hundred Years War (1338-1453) contributed to the fourteenth century population retrogression (East, 1966: 78). This took place in such a way that the population surviving the

---

[22] Itself due possibly to the fact that bastards some places were born free and in these places it was in the manorial lord's interest to maximize the legitimate population.

pestilences of the fourteenth century was unevenly
distributed (Hilton, 1973: 16-17). A second major feature
of the fourteenth century, viewed alongside the demographic
changes in the 1300s, signalled the beginning of the end of
the feudal era. Class struggles, particularly as they
resulted in significant emigration from the feudal estates
(or the threat of such movement), contributed to the later
re-emergence of a free peasantry, the development of rural
wage labor, and the growth of the towns. Let me introduce
the class struggles at the height of the feudal period and
the concomitant alterations in peasant migrations and their
impact upon class formation.

Maurice Dobb (1963: 50ff), in a survey of the ruling
class response to the population decline, recognizes that
the feudal peasantry was met with two types of situation:
concessions and a mitigation of the servile burden; or firm
measures designed to maintain or increase the extraction of
surplus product through the continued imposition of
traditional feudal social relations of production. The
latter option was "most marked and most successful" (Dobb,
1963: 51) in Eastern Europe under German rule and in Spain.
"There was even some revival of the slave trade in the
Mediterranean to supply landowners with cultivators" (Dobb,
1963: 51). It was in these areas in which peasant struggles
and the migratory movements (which set the stage for

capitalist production elsewhere) were most harnessed that the "feudal reaction" was most evident. While it was a "progressive" Spanish ruling class which may have advanced primitive accumulation through the plunder of the Americas, it was a reactionary Spanish ruling class which virtually enslaved those Jews and Moslems who had not been driven from the continent. The German advance into Eastern Europe and the Baltic may have introduced feudal social relations of production into areas with less well developed economies but feudalism was elsewhere (France and England) revealing its limitations. However it is the first option of the feudal ruling class which interests us here: the liberalization of feudal relations between the ruling class and the peasantry. It was this response, especially in Britain, which accelerated the dissolution of feudalism.

Let me examine in more detail the pertinent developments in the English countryside--as England was the site of the first massive and permanent capitalist system of production. The key factors are peasant-landlord class struggles, the relaxation of restrictions on peasant mobility along with growth of factors which drove the peasantry from the land, and the increased tendency toward money rents.

The fourteenth century saw some dramatic events which signalled and accelerated the collapse of the feudal system. Foremost among these were the plagues of 1349, the 1360s, and the 1370s as well as revolts which shook various parts of Europe. While the French Jacquerie of 1358; the Italian risings of 1310, 1313, and 1318; and the Flanders revolt of 1323-27 are notable, the English rising of 1381 is of particular interest here. This somewhat mis-named "Peasants' Revolt" was symptomatic of the contradictions which had been slowly developing in English feudal society.

I have already mentioned the growth of population in the centuries immediately preceding the fourteenth and the stresses population growth brought about within the feudal system. The episodes of pestilence in the fourteenth century, however, not only contributed to a remission in population growth, but initiated regionally and in many towns a depopulation with which the existing system of land tenure and labor organization was unable to cope. Not only did population pressure collapse, but so too, did the settlement movement, which population growth helped cause and fuelled.

This brings up the role of population in the demise of the feudal mode of production. Was population retrogression, the widespread mortality and suffering, itself a sufficient condition for the downfall of feudalism? This was the traditional interpretation with the implied hypothesis that somehow the social disruption and psychological impact of widespread disease, famine, and death contributed to social disorganization. This explanation is now given little credence as I shall discuss at a later point. The explanation I pursue, at least partial explanation, is that migration played an important role.

Hypothesis Two

Colonial resettlement before the fourteenth century population crisis established a pattern of population distribution which could not withstand, within homeostatic limits, the population retrogression.

Discussion

Forms of corporate migration prior to the Black Death, the settlement movement in particular, established population size near the upper limits of the homeostatic carrying capacity. This could not be maintained in the face of the population crisis. I argue that migration following the fourteenth century crisis period did not, in itself, contribute to the downfall of feudalism. It was the period of migration before the crisis which helped prepare the demographic deathbed of feudalism.

In subsequent chapters, I argue that migration after the fourteenth century contributed instead to the rise of

capitalism, if the demise of feudalism may be separated
from the rise of capitalism, at least theoretically. In
the remainder of this chapter I shall pursue the hypothesis
that migration was the demographic means by which
socio-economic stability was maintained in the face of
environmental factors which tended to increase actual
population size. By examining the political upheaval which
accompanied the crisis period, I demonstrate the legacy of
the settlement movement.

Fourteenth Century Class Struggles

The population crisis disrupted the flow of seignorial
and royal income. It might well also have accelerated the
peasant and artisan quest for greater freedom--especially
as cultivable land became increasingly available due to
high mortality among the cultivators. Moreover, with the
shortage of labor, wages began to rise.[23] Two forms of
state intervention in this situation helped to perpetuate
the class struggles (among other violent manifestations) of
the 1381 uprising: taxation and the Statutes of Labourers.
Dobson (1970: 51) and Hilton (1973: chapter 5) are in
agreement on these and the plague as contributing to the
revolt. Additionally, Hilton (1973: 145) has noted that the

---

[23] Wage labor, of course, was still not the norm. Serf
labor commonly experienced lighter dues in England.

disturbances tended to take place in "the areas of densest population, of most complete manorialization and of production for the market [footnote deleted]." These factors illustrate three problems disrupting the feudal system: abrupt and uneven population change, uneven persistance of feudal oppression, and the intrusion of market forces.

The rising itself (see the chronologies of the events in Hilton, 1973: 137-143 or in Dobson, 1970: 36-48) consisted of a series of rebellions mainly near and in London, the southeast of England, and East Anglia. More than two dozen communities were involved; most of the action was in the summer of 1381. The spark which ignited the revolt (evidently first in Essex) was the imposition of the third poll tax in four years. Taxation was the pre-eminent underlying factor throughout the rebellious areas. In addition, a variety of grievences, both by peasants with the local feudal establishment and by peasants and artisans with the state, were contributing factors in the specific communities involved.

The latest taxation, a series of poll taxes designed to support the Hundred Years War between England and France (the war itself a vain attempt by England to retain possessions in France), was but one of the oppressive periods of taxation in the fourteenth century. In 1334, for example, the taxation of villages was fixed in lump sums such that with the high mortality of 1349, the average peasant's assessment increased (Hilton, 1973: 148). One contemporary observer, Thomas Walsingham, described the first (1377) poll tax as "a hitherto unheard-of-tax" (Dobson, 1970: 103). By the time of the second poll tax (1379), tax evasion was so effective as to cause official complaint of revenue shortages so with the third poll tax (enacted late 1380), tax collector John Leg and three colleagues devised a means of enforcing collection, related by Henry Knighton in the contemporary Anomimalle Chronicle cited in Dobson (1970: 135):

> One of these commissioners came to a certain village to investigate the said tax and called together the men and the women; he then, horrible to relate, shamelessly lifted the young girls to test whether they had enjoyed intercourse with men. In this way he compelled the friends and parents of these girls to pay the tax for them: many would rather pay for their daughters than see them touched in such a disgraceful way. These and similar actions by the said inquisitors much provoked the people.

The point to be made here with regard to the taxation policies which touched off the 1381 rising is that population related policy (the attempt to maintain conquests of French lands and peoples) and population phenomena (widespread mortality due to the series of plagues) were among the immediate causes of England's first class-based, multi-regional political debacle. The poll tax is one example of the impact of the state upon the masses who rose up in 1381. Another form of state intervention consisted of attempts at freezing wages beginning with the Ordinance of Labourers (1349) and Statute of Labourers (1351). But unlike the system of taxation which was imposed by the king upon both commoners and gentry, the Statutes of Labourers (both the 1349 and 1351 legislation) were imposed by Parliament (representing the landlords) upon the poorest section of the peasantry which lacked sufficient land to subsist without engaging in wage labor. Moreover, the legislation was enforced by "a great lord . . . [and] members of the gentry. some with legal training, and all identifiable with the interests of lords of manors" (Hilton, 1973: 154). While it would appear that the statutes were unsuccessful in their purpose of maintaining cheap labor by rolling wages back to the pre-plague level of 1346, they must have sufficiently antagonized the laboring classes such that the Statutes of Labourers also contributed to the class struggles of 1381. "Many such justices [charged with inforcing the statutes] were the target of attack in 1381; and it can be no coincidence that the risings of that year tended to be most violent in those counties where it is known the hated labour laws were strictly enforced" (Dobson, 1970: 69).

How does one square Dobson's observation on the target
of attack (justices who sought to keep wage rates low in
the face of labor scarcity) with Hilton's observation that
the revolts took place in densely populated areas? Two
ways. First, we must not accept at face value the inference
that the Statutes of Labourers were enacted and enforced
simply and solely to maintain manorial financial
equilibrium in the face of population decline. (Why was
there need to impose oppressive measures in densely
populated areas where, presumable, labor scarcity did not
contribute to higher wages?) Secondly, we must avoid the
temptation to adopt demographic determinism. (Evidently
population density was not the sole factor determining wage
rates.) Hilton noted not only the population density of
the areas of revolt but also their degrees of
manorialization and production for the market. This meshes
nicely with Dobson's (1970: 12) historiographical comment:

> Sixty years ago the late fourteenth century was
> commonly viewed as a decisive watershed in the
> social, political, and religious history of
> England. The Black Death, the Peasants' Revolt,
> the emergence of Wycliffe and Chaucer seemed to
> mark the dawn of a genuinely new era. . . . 'the
> meeting place of the medieval and modern'. Few
> present day historians would dare claim as much.
> According to the modern orthodoxy, the
> catastrophic onslaught of bubonic plague . . .
> merely accelerated social and economic forces
> already fully evident in early fourteenth century
> England.

My interpretation of this important conjuncture suggests
that while destabalizing for a time, the 1381 revolt
represented a crystallization[24] of the class formation
of feudal England already in decline.

The 1381 rising has commonly been called the
"Peasants' Revolt" though its participants were of artisan
as well as peasant origin; some were members of the clergy;
a very few were members of the gentry. According to Hilton
(1973: 184) "The social composition of the rebellious bands
reflected the stratification of contemporary society." And
while there were clearly elements of class conflict in the
uprising, Hilton (1973: 184) seems to stress the division
of the "mass of the population" from "the lords, the
lawyers and government officials." On the basis of what is
known about the actual events, this is undoubtably correct.
I hasten to add, however, that it was a rebellion against
the feudal state apparatus by oppresed elements from the
past (the serfs) as well as the nascent urban artisans. The
class analysis I propose here is made possible largely by
the events recorded in 1381. These events appeared at that
particular conjuncture because the productive and market

---

[24] By "crystallization" I mean to suggest that the
class antagonisms underlying English feudalism were brought
into perspective, this perspective being refracted
through the observations of contemporaries and
historians, to reveal a concrete record of the feudal
social structure.

forces within the English towns, alongside traditional
peasant production in the wake of high mortality, came into
conflict with the social relations of feudal production and
oppression. Those attempts by the feudal ruling class to
tighten its grip upon the productive classes (similar in
direction to those which refeudalized Eastern Europe) were
met with opposition by both the traditional
agriculturalists and their emergent counterparts in the
medieval towns: urban opponents such as the "carpenters,
sawyers, masons, cobblers, tailors, weavers, fullers,
glovers, hosiers, skiners, bakers, butchers, innkeepers,
cooks, and a lime burner" who were indicted in the Kentish
revolt (Hilton, 1973: 179). Townspeople were, however, in
the minority.

The major thrust of the peasants' revolt was a drive
from the rural villages to the towns and finally a march on
London. While most of the dissident activities remained
localized, the power of the central government was duly
recognized by the rebels and their decisive defeat was at
the hands of the king at the edge of London. The political
role of the city vis-a-vis the countryside was clearly
evident in the 1381 revolt. But the economic role of the
city--London in particular--as dominant over the
countryside had yet to be manifested. Urban economic
hegemony was not to be fully operative until the emergence

of widespread capitalist production in subsequent centuries.

Accompanying the emergence of the city as the center of economic activities was a shift in the patterns of population movement. From the settlement of rural waste lands and the extension of cultivation at the height of the feudal period, movement to the population centers came to characterize internal migration in the darkness before the dawn of capitalism in England.

In summary, I have suggested that prior to 1349, migration had been a key factor in the tendency of population to increase to near the upper limit of the homeostatic carrying capacity. In the following century, exogenous environmental factors (especially the plague) acted upon population to increase mortality, causing a drastic drop in population. The various feudal responses to this population retrogression, especially in Britain, contributed to class conflict and structural change within feudal society.

CHAPTER VI

URBANIZATION AND POPULATION MOVEMENT IN EARLY MODERN
ENGLAND

Introduction

The major issue considered in this chapter is the
conjuncture of three factors which appeared in fourteenth
century England and which set the stage for the subsequent
development of the industrial revolution and capitalist
production. These three factors were: 1. population
trends; 2. state intervention; and 3. the emergent class
formation of English cities. Had any one of these not
appeared in a timely manner, capitalist production might
have been forestalled to another time or place. Moreover,
even if these or similar factors appeared elsewhere,
additional intervening factors could have been responsible
for their failure to congeal into a system capable of
supporting capitalist production. Theoretically speaking,
England was not the inevitable birthplace of capitalism; a
setting which would encourage the development of the
prerequisites of capitalism may well have been present

elsewhere only to have formed at a later date or to have developed more slowly.

Hypothesis Three

Socio-economic reprganization after the fourteenth century population crisis established a lower population homeostasis.

Discussion

The central hypothesis developed in this chapter is that a structural change in class formation and in the class dimension of state intervention into peasant affairs took place in the context of a socio-economic reorganization which effected the establishment of population homeostasis at a lower, post-crisis level.

My argument is that in the attempt to retain feudal authority following the social disorder brought on by the decimation of population, various types of reorganization of both production (serf-land bond) and politics (lord-serf bond) took place which had the short-term effect of maintaining feudalism but the long-term effect of introducing a re-ordering of society which undermined feudal production and authority. The specific processes I address are the impact of state intervention into peasant mobility, urbanization, and the enclosure movement.

Population, Labor, and State Intervention

In the previous chapter I outlined the migratory response to the steady increase in population which was reversed in the fourteenth century. The population increase was characterized throughout Europe by the extension of cultivation and the establishment of new settlements. The direct impact of the contraction in population (aside from its general decimation) is less certain. In England, essentially two patterns seem to have appeared: the total desertion of villages and population reduction in many additional towns. Archeological and other evidence shows clearly that the first took place; Hoskins (1976: 93) attributes it to the plague, though I am more inclined to follow Beresford (1954: 99-100, 158ff; Beresford and Hurst, 1971: 9-10) in discounting this. The plague probably totally depopulated some villages (or rendered them unviable due to high mortality), though the plague alone was probably not responsible for a great many of the lost villages (Beresford, 1954: 202). The main impact of the fourteenth century pestilences upon village population, I would say, was a much more severe reduction of population in some villages than in others thus causing localized labor shortages.

Many fourteenth century total village depopulations which took place, I suggest, may have been due in no small part to state interventions. The means of final total depopulation of certain villages was likely due to emigration following an episode of high mortality. Here is the argument: In 1334 (prior to any of the catastrophic epidemics), a tax was levied upon all English villages--not a head tax but a village tax. We know that some villages were assessed more heavily than others while a few were even exempted from taxation. It was those with the lightest assessments which suffered the highest rates of desertion (Beresford and Hurst, 1971: 20ff.) The scheme of village tax assessment and tax relief was intended to reflect relative wealth. However, if the assessments were none the less disproportionately heavy on the poorest of villages, that could have driven residents of these villages into flight to neighboring towns with tax assessments more proportionate to the villagers' abilities to pay. Since Beresford and Hurst (1971: 20ff) also found a correlation between the size of the village and its demise (the smaller were more likely to disappear), the taxation could have been effectively higher on a per capita basis in the smaller vills, if my general argument is correct, possibly because of an explicit or implicit minimum village tax. Another possibility is that economies

of scale operated such that larger villages could afford
higher per capita taxes. The first poll tax of 1377 might
well have accelerated the flight from certain villages.
Indeed, Beresford's (1954: 162-63) study of these tax
assessments finds that in each, the "to-be-lost" villages
had lower assessments. Unfortunately, surviving records do
not allow for an estimate of the actual number of villages
which vanished between 1334 and 1377 (Beresford, 1954:
163-64).

The Statutes of Laborers enacted in the fourteenth
century, as I mentioned in chapter five, were intended to
limit wages. Another purpose, however, was to restrict
peasant and artisan migration. Legislation of 1388 known
as the "Statute of 12 Richard II" (cited in Bland, Brwn,
and Tawney, 1914: 172) illustrates this point:

> . . . no servant or laborer, be it man or woman,
> depart at the end of his term out of the hundred,
> rape or wapentake where he is dwelling, to serve
> or dwell elsewhere, or by color of going afar on
> pilgramage, unless he carry a letter patent
> containing the cause of his going and the time of
> his return . . . and any servant or laborer be
> found in a city, borough or elswhere, coming from
> any place, wandering without such letter, he
> shall be taken forthwith by the said mayors,
> bailiffs, stewards or constables and put in
> stocks . . .

While it is not clear that such passages were rigorously
enforced (for what mayor, bailiff, steward, or constable
would punish job-seekers where there was a labor

shortage?), it is clear that both the Parliament and the King, in this period, introduced measures which tended to heighten the oppression of the laboring masses. Moreover, the need the ruling classes felt for state control of peasant mobility indicates that something was amiss within the traditional feudal organization of labor.

Enclosures and Migration

The enclosure of agriculture lands with hedges and dikes to keep livestock from straying took place for a lengthy period in England. Enclosures and resulting village depopulations appeared at least as early as the eleventh century, initiated by clerical sects such as the Cistercians. While these monks were said to desire privacy, thus the enclosure of monastic lands, it is important to note that the enclosed lands were used for pasture (Beresford and Hurst, 1971: 6). Enclosure was one means of village depopulation and displacement of peasant families which continued through the ages. The fourteenth century contraction of the population probably facilitated enclosure to some degree for ordinarily it was an extremely unpopular practice among those who were not enclosers.

One main reason for the change from arable to pastoral farming, according to Beresford (1954: passim; Beresford and Hurst, 1971: 13-14), was the price-change differentials between corn and wool. From 1450 (the earliest date for which price series are available) till 1600, there were eight periods in which the price increases of wool and grain alternated with the lead of one over the other. For example, for the period 1462-1486, wool prices rose by 29% over their earlier prices of 1450-1461 while grain prices fell by 2% over the same period, giving wool an ascendency index of 31% (29% minus a negative 2%). Grain attained ascendency (17%) in the 1486-1502 period; wool (10%) in 1503-1517; grain (40%) in 1518-1535; wool (17%) in 1536-1547; grain (59%) in 1548-1572; wool (6%) in 1573-1583; and grain (35%) in 1584- 1600 (Beresford and Hurst, 1971: 12-14, especially Figure 1, p. 13). While it is clear that overall grain prices increased more than did wool (1450-1600), those periods in which wool prices rose faster than grain may well have encouraged some farmers to shift from corn to sheep thus requiring land enclosure. Even if many of these farmers shifted back to grain in times of grain price ascendency, there would not necessarily be need of levelling the hedges.

The sheep droppings fertilized the soil and contributed to the higher productivity of enclosed (formerly sheep) lands vis-a-vis open fields. If the landholders who enclosed for sheep rearing were generally more inclined towards innovation than the predominately conservative peasantry, this group would likely have been responsible for field rotation, changes in the organization of labor (especially the use of wage labor), and the introduction of new technology (e.g. the horse-drawn plow). These in totality contributed to the higher yield of enclosed lands over open fields, especially since the older techniques associated with open fields required that a portion of the land remain fallow--unnecessary with crop rotation and manure use.

The question arises: If enclosed fields were really so superior to open fields, why were enclosures so unpopular among both the peasantry and the ruling class which is known to have legislated against and prosecuted enclosers? The answer to the first lies in the population displacement and associated misery suffered by the peasantry; the answer to the second is a separate political and economic issue which shall be discussed later in this chapter.

We have no way of knowing with great accuracy the extent of enclosures, how many peasants were forced to emigrate from their ancestral homelands, why they took place where they did and when, etc. Most of what we know comes from trials of enclosers, archeology and landscape surveys, and political tracts which have survived the centuries. Examination of current landscapes, old maps, and ruins indicates that the most drastic enclosures took

place before 1488. Later enclosures did not usually totally
depopulate villages. Those which did, especially between
1450 and 1486, probably did so because of the economies of
scale in sheep rearing--it did not make economic sense to
enclose only portions of villages' open fields. The total
depopulation of which we have evidence as of 1486 may not
have been caused solely by enclosures. As noted in chapter
five, the total village depopulations took place in
villages already decimated by pestilence or taxation. The
smallest villages were most susceptable to total
depopulation (Beresford and Hurst, 1971: 11-20). While the
worst of total depopulations took place before 1485, most
of the total depopulations had taken place by 1517, and the
last took place later in the same century. Partial village
depopulation continued into the 17th century (Beresford,
1954: 141-150). "By the end of the seventeenth century
enclosure for sheep had spent its force," according to
Gregg (1976: 175), who added that "with thousands of
deserted villages, new arable land had been broken in on
the northern hills and moorland, . . ." Moreover, "some
three-fifths of the cultivated land of England and Wales
was still unenclosed by the middle of the eighteenth
century, . . ." (Gregg, 1976: 176).

Gregg's observations raise and partially answer the
question of what happened to the displaced population. Some

peasants entered into the cultivation of lands opened up by the clearing of forests and the draining of moorlands, increasing arable land by ten percent (Hill, 1969: 152). There were several major differences between this period of clearing and the earlier one which occurred throughout Europe. For one thing, in the second clearing period innovations in technique and technology predominated while innovations in the feudal relations of production were most important earlier. There was greater secondary displacement or disruption of the population living in the lands to be cleared or drained in the later clearing movement.

It is well known, however, that not all peasants displaced by enclosures were able to migrate to clear new land. Many had no choice but to simply move on--a period of itinerancy, if not vagrancy, often preceeded the taking-up of city residence or emigration to the colonies. In the period before the industrial revolution, the enclosures are probably responsible for much of the urbanization. Moreover, there is likely to have been higher fertility in the rural areas than in the cities (especially London) thus the urban-rural fertility differentials may have acted as an antecedent variable triggering migration to the cities. Migration was clearly much more important for the cities' growth than the urban rate of natural increase, given high rates of urban mortality.

It takes little imagination to understand why the
peasants were opposed to enclosure. Several radical peasant
movements were associated with opposition to enclosure. The
Levellers favored the levelling of hedges and the return to
open-field arable farming, among other social issues. The
Diggers were, in Gregg's (1976: 182) words, "simple
agrarian communists." The Diggers' leader in 1649, Gerrard
Winstanley, according to Gregg (1976: 180, original source
cited: Gerrard Winstanley, The New Law of Righteousness,
January, 1649),

> instructed his followers that the Lord 'wil have
> us that are called common people, to manure and
> work upon the common lands'. 'No man', he said,
> 'shall have any more land than he can labour
> himself, or have others to labour with him in
> love' . . . If the rich, he said, 'hold fast this
> property of Mine and Thine, let them labour their
> own Land with their own hands. And let the
> common-people, that say the earth is ours, not
> mine, let them labour together, and eat bread
> together upon the Commons, Mountains, and Hils'.

The Levellers and the Diggers both participated in the
rhetoric of the Civil War. Their ideologies suggest that
the peasants wanted little more than to continue farming
much as they had or thought they (as a class) had in the
past. Notwithstanding an otherworldly idealism among some
groups, why did their protagonists, the feudal lords, also
oppose enclosure for such a long time?

The ruling class is even better able to speak for
itself in historical matters. After all, history is

usually ruling-class history--records of the ruling class
are better kept and more available. Essentially, the feudal
lords were at first opposed to enclosure not only because
were they conservative but they (understandably) opposed
any economic innovation which threatened the existing
balance of class power. As the feudal system decayed and
the balance tipped toward the bourgeois elements within the
ruling class, enclosure came to be seen for what it was as
an economic force: a movement which bolstered the national
economy by increasing the output of the rural sector while
providing cheap labor for the emergent industrial sector.

Among the earliest (1236-37) records of judicial
proceedings treating enclosure as cited in Bland, Brown,
and Tawney (1914: 89; original source: Bracton's
Note-book), one enclosure was allowed and one disallowed,
each seemingly based upon fairness and customary practice.
In the disallowed enclosure, Adam de Bladewrthe charged
that Robert de Fislake "unjustly raised a dyke in Woodhouse
to the injury of the free tenement of Adam . . ."

> The jurors say that the aforesaid Adam always
> used to have common in that meadow and in the
> land of Robert by that meadow after the corn and
> hay were carried, and when the land lay fallow,
> then in both meadow and fallow, and Robert caused
> the meadow to be enclosed so that Adam can have
> no entry to that pasture. And so it is awarded
> that the dyke be thrown down, and the meadow made
> as it should be, so that the aforesaid Adam have
> entry and issue, and that Robert be in mercy,
> etc.

In another action, the court allowed Elias of Leyburn to cultivate a certain wood, formerly held in common, because of an intervening covenant which allowed for the partition of the land in question among five lords. The right to common herbage after the corn was harvested, as was allowed in the covenant, was retained. These admittedly isolated examples were early indications of the ruling class position on enclosure which was not to prevail until four centuries later. Common law as opposed to feudal custom came to decide land questions by the seventeenth century.

The opposition to enclosure came to be increasingly founded upon its disruption of the decaying feudal economy. In particular, enclosure opponents presented arguments which in retrospect we see had important class implications. For example, legislation[25] enacted in 1533-34 was aimed at limiting to 2000 the number of sheep "those greedy and covetous people" (the enclosers) may keep "at any one time within any part of this realm of all sorts and kinds, upon pain to lose and forfeit for every sheep that any person shall have or keep above the number limited by this act, 3s. 4d. . . . ." The economic impact of this penalty upon the greedy and covetous as well as some rationale for the act is illustrated by a passage in the

---

[25] "An Act Concerning Farms and Sheep," reprinted in Bland, Brown, and Tawney (1914: 264-266.)

same legislation which indicated the increase in price: "a good sheep for victual that was accustomed to be sold for 2s. 4d. or 3s. at the most, is sold now for 6s., 5s. or 4s. at the least; . . ." Another (Bland, Brown, and Tawney, 1914: 268-70) against enclosure stresed the human impact, holding enclosures responsible for having

> raised and enhanced the prices of all manner of corn, cattle, wool, pigs, geese, hens, chickens, eggs and such other almost double above the prices which hath been accustomed, by reason whereof a marvellous multitude and number of people of this realm be not able to provide meat, drink and clothes necessary for themselves, their wives and children, but be so discouraged with misery and poverty that they fall daily to theft, robbery and other inconvenience, or pitifully die for hunger and cold;

In 1549, by an Act of the Privy Council, attempts were made to remedy the problems caused by enclosure in the town of Godmanchester by requiring the restoration of the right of habitation of vacant houses, reforestation of woods cleared for pasture, and the construction of alternative housing if houses vacated by enclosure eviction were put to other use ("Intervention of Privy Council under Somerset to Protect Tenants," in Bland, Brown, and Tawney, 1914: 266-268). But within a century the tables had turned on the enclosure opponents.

While "An Act for the Maintenance of Husbandry and Tillage" (Bland, Brown, and Tawney, 1914: 268-270), speaking for the opponents of enclosure in 1597-98, cited

the social reasons for, and called for a return to tillage
as opposed to pasture, it also made reference to
legislation enacted four years earlier, "since which time
there have grown many more depopulations, by turning
tillage into pasture, than at any time for the like number
of years heretofore . . ." Opposition to enclosure within
the government continued at least through the seventeenth
century, though by the end of the sixteenth, the
pro-enclosure forces were close to making their position
prevail in Parliament for the first time.

According to Professor Hill, "the famine year 1597 saw
the last acts against depopulation; 1608 the first
(limited) pro-enclosure act" (Hill, 1969: 69). By 1640, the
anti-enclosure M.P.s had been sufficiently diminished in
numbers to be ineffective, though enclosures and
pro-enclosure laws continued to be met with Parliamentary
and peasant opposition at least until that time. "Enclosure
fines became an irregular tax levied on one section of the
landed class, and gave no adequate protection to the poor"
(Hill, 1969: 69).

Urbanization

Urbanization may best illustrate the power and
flexibility of migration as a demographic means of
correcting for departures from population homeostasis. It
is generally accepted that in pre-modern times, urban
growth (urbanization) was due more to in-migration than to
the rate of natural increase. This phenomenon, and the
flexibility of migration vis-a-vis fertility in re-stocking
a locality which has experienced a sudden population
decrease, are illustrated by comparing London's recovery
from the fourteenth century plagues with that of the whole
country. The population of England was nearly halved, from
about three and three-quarters million in the middle of the
fourteenth century to about two million by the beginning of
the fifteenth century (Russell, 1948: 280). The
population of London was diminished by some forty thousand
during the 1348-49 plague, which must have been a large
part of its population. London's estimated population as
late as 1300 was only forty thousand--unchanged from 1200
(Chandler and Fox, 1974: 137). However, by 1377, London's
population had returned to about thirty-five thousand and
by the turn of the century had reached forty-five thousand,
according to Chandler and Fox's (1974: 137) estimates.
Even allowing for some population growth in the first half

of the fourteenth century, and even if Chandler and Fox's estimate is high (the 1377 poll tax counted 23,314 adults), the apparant recovery is remarkable considering the two centuries it took the country as a whole to return to its pre-plague population size.

The restocking of the cities may have actually delayed the national population recovery. Here is the argument. The cities had lower rates of natural increase due in no small part to higher mortality--cummunicable diseases were more easily spread in the crowded and unsanitary cities and urban residents had less direct access to food supplies. Without net migration between the cities and the countryside, the cities would be expected to lose an even greater proportion of their populations than rural areas and take longer to return to the original population. And cities probably lost proportionatly more population, but some, e.g. London, seemed to rebound much more rapidly than the national population. This suggests that numbers of people who should have constituted a substantial part of the rural population increase were consumed, instead, in the cities.

If London's recovery was remarkable, its general rate of growth, compared to the period of the industrial revolution, was much less so. The population of london increased from 40,000 in 1400 to 861,000 in 1800, but

London's population grew to about 2,320,000 in the
following half-century. While it is true that much of the
earlier increase took place between 1600 and 1800, the
second period (1800-50) was a veritable exponential
increase.[26] What was it that sustained London's rate of
growth?

Basically four factors were involved in the growth of
London in the early modern period. For one, London was the
seat of government. This is true also of Constantinople,
Peking, and Paris--the other major world cities in this
period. Secondly, like the others, London was an important
commercial center. Third, as is also the case for such
dominant cities (particularly those associated with the
advanced communal mode of production), the surplus product
extracted from the peasantry by pre-capitalist means tended
to be consumed by an urban-based ruling class. Feudalism,
however, differed from the advanced communal mode of
production. Under feudalism, consumption of the social
surplus took place in both the cities and the countryside.
That wealth which was immediately absorbed by residents of
the feudal cities, as was also the case among the advanced

---

[26] Such growth of pre-capitalist cities is not unheard
of: Constantinople (which fell from its Byzantine peak
of some half to one million in the eleventh century)
grew from about 50,000 in 1450 to about 700,000 by 1600
as capital of the Ottoman Empire, though it leveled off
and even declined until the early nineteenth century.
See the Chandler and Fox (1974: 175-176) estimates.

communal cities, was used to sustain the urban population
and its ceremonies. In England, however, some capital was
accumulated in the rural areas, not reaching the cities
until opportunities for investment appeared. The fourth
factor, therefore, was the second-stage flow of wealth from
the villages to the cities, which took place within a
proto-capitalist setting in London (and Paris).
Contemporaneous with the population explosion of London in
the late eighteenth and nineteenth centuries was a
similar--though much smaller in numbers--expansion of
population in other English cities: Manchester, Liverpool,
Birmingham, Leeds, Bristol, Sheffield, Newcastle,
Wolverhampton, Plymouth, and Bradford had all reached or
surpassed the 100,000 mark by 1850 (Chandler and Fox, 1974:
133-140).

Let me explore some theoretical reasons for a
seemingly exponential rate of urbanization. To utilize the
homeostatic model, one must explain the rapid population
growth by changes in environmental and/or socio-economic
factors. We can probably rule out any environmental change
of a magnitude which would constitute the sole or main
cause of exponential population increase. (Of course
disease or natural disaster could cause an exponential
decrease in population.) This leaves social (including
political) and economic factors. Utilizing the nation as

the unit of analysis, some additional light may be shed
upon the issue.

If the political situation changes such that a strong
government is established in a city where little political
and military power was to be found immediately prior to the
conjuncture in question, one could easily imagine
conditions which might encourage rapid population growth.
Soldiers, administrators, the court, the clergy, servants,
merchants, tradespeople, and many other categories of
residents would likely be attracted to the seat of power.
The size of this largely non-productive population would be
limited to that which could be supported by the extraction
of the surplus of the productive population of the
hinterland. In the pre-capitalist epoch, the productivity
of agriculture--within the limits of the specific mode of
production, environment, technology, and social class
relationships[27] would define the maximum size of the
non-productive (urban) population. Therefore, one means of
effecting a seemingly (but self-limiting) exponential rate
of urban growth, would be the establishment of a strong
central government. This likely explains the repopulation
of Constantinople under the Ottomans. The growing
political power of London may also help to explain London's

---

[27] Especially the ability of the ruling class to
extract the surplus from the hinterland.

population increase. Similar arguments could also be made for Paris, Peking, and a host of other cities which experienced rapid population increases. Such an explanation, however, is not likely to hold for the many other English cities which also experienced seeming, though smaller-scale, exponential rates of growth with the industrial revolution.

In retrospect, we know now that the rapid urbanization which took place in Britain in the nineteenth century took place at a time when the industrial capital stage of the capitalist mode of production had come to dominate the English nation. Therefore, one could hypothesize that changes from one mode of production to another (especially from a pre-capitalist to the capitalist), or major structural metamorphosis within a mode of production (in this case from mercantilism to industrialization), may be associated with profound demographic changes. We are fairly certain that much of the urbanization (especially its initial stages) was due to in-migration. Therefore, if I am to suggest a causal sequence of events, it would be circular. That is, urbanization was caused by economic and demographic changes which drove some elements of the rural population to the cities. The driving force was the disintegration of the feudal mode of production through the enclosure movement and social changes which affected fertility and migration. The development of capitalism which took place with the dissolution of feudalism enabled the cities to absorb a large productive population--in contrast to the mainly non-productive populations of pre-capitalist cities. The economic demands of the cities, therefore, came to draw increasing numbers of workers from the countryside. The rapid urbanization which marked the industrial revolution is a classic example of the symbiotic operation of push and pull migration.

Urbanization, Economy, and the Dissolution of Feudalism

Urban development plays an important role in any discussion of the transition from feudalism to capitalism. In a study of international labor migration, we are especially interested in cities insofar that they have constituted the spatial loci of capital accumulation and industrial capitalism. As such, and by the very nature of urbanization, cities have been the destinations of individual migrants as well as identifiable migration streams--international and internal. Therefore, in order to highlight the bourgeois and working classes which peopled the late medieval cities and provided the human fuel for subsequent capitalist development, I look at the urban political economy before the industrial revolution in Britain.

In a well-known essay on the city, Max Weber (1976: 21) stressed the roles of the market place and of urban production: "We wish to speak of a 'city' only in cases where the local inhabitants satisfy an economically substantial part of their daily wants in the local market, and to an essential extent by products which the local populations and that of the immediate hinterland produced for sale in the market or acquired in other ways". The existence of cities (in the Weberian sense) certainly characterized England on the eve of the industrial revolution. One is tempted to suggest that the presence of one or more such cities is a necessary, if not sufficient precondition of capitalism. After all, one is hard-presssed to think of a country which has developed a modern (i.e. industrial) capitalist economy without at least one city, though any number of cities were historically at least as advanced as (if not more so than) London--in the Low Countries or Northern Italy, for example.

There are for our purposes two related, but distinct, analytical points of departure which bear upon the understanding of the role of cities in the development of capitalism. These two, and they are also useful in understanding migration, are often identified with Sweezy (1978), and Dobb (1963). I shall first briefly summarize

the two respective positions and then develop the analysis
(something of a synthesis of these) in the light of the
political economy of urban England before the industrial
revolution.

Sweezy (1978a) published his original essay in
question in a 1950 issue of Science and Society as a
critique of Dobb's Studies in the Development of Capitalism
(1963) which was first published in 1946. From that first
shot at Dobb sprang a lengthy exchange among Dobb and his
supporters vis-a-vis Sweezy. Rodney Hilton (1978)
subsequently published a reprint of the series of debates
in The Transition from Feudalism to Capitalism. The
following discussion will be based primariliy upon the Dobb
(1963) and Hilton (1978) books.

While urban development is not a central concern of
Sweezy, he is associated with the variant explanation of
capitalism which focuses upon the market place--especially
in the context of international trade. Sweezy's position
on the primary factor underlying the development of
feudalism is that, crudely speaking, long distance trade
served as an external factor which corroded the feudal
social and economic structure thus causing its downfall.
While Sweezy is quick to admit that in reality it was a
complex of internal and external factors operating together
which brought down the English feudal structure (1978b:

104), my understanding of Sweezy's position is that (urban-centered) long-distance trade is not only a necessary, but a sufficient condition for the dissolution of feudal society. This is because of the role of trade in altering the consumption patterns of the ruling class, causing it to accumulate as well as consume. The result of this lengthy process of altering consumption was the heightened exploitation of the peasantry which, along with other factors such as population growth, reached its limits within the constraints of the feudal organization of production. Simply speaking, the need of the ruling class for increased revenue could not be met by the existing feudal organization of production. According to Sweezy (1978a: 41 n. 10): "the growth of trade was the decisive factor in bringing about the decline of western European feudalism." At risk of oversimplifying Sweezy's argument, I think Sweezy would agree that one crucial difference between feudalism and capitalism lies in the arrangement of productive-consumption: feudal lords consume goods and services at the end of the production process while capitalist consumption serves to accumulate and extend production, not to end it. Sweezy then would likely agree that the medieval cities, as the loci of trade and (later) surplus population, intruded upon and irrevocably altered the feudal patterns of consumption. As to the role of

migration (we are speaking here of rural-urban migration),
Sweezy writes: "the flight of the serfs took place
simultaneousely with the growth of the towns, especially in
the 12th and 13th centuries. There is no doubt that the
rapidly developing towns--offering, as they did, liberty,
employment and improved social status--acted as a powerful
magnet to the oppressed rural population" (1978a: 40).

Dobb and his followers, it would seem, see a
fundamental difference between the Sweezy and Dobb
positions. Dobb finds within the fabric of rural feudal
society the seeds of its own destruction. Anticipating
Sweezy's later critique, Dobb acknowledges the importance
of increased trade (from the twelfth century), in
connection with the intensification of feudal labor
obligations and serf labor extractions, as a standard
interpretation of western feudal history (Dobb, 1963:
37-38). According to Dobb (1963: 38):

> What is questionable, however, is whether the
> connection was as simple and direct as has often
> been depicted, and whether the widening of the
> market can be held to have been a <u>sufficient</u>
> condition for the decline of Feudalism--whether
> an explanation is possible in terms of this as
> the sole or even the decisive factor. . . .
> "Natural economy" and "exchange economy" are two
> economic orders that cannot mix, and the presence
> of the latter, we are told, is sufficient to
> cause the former to go into dissolution.
> [Emphasis in the original.]

Already in his Studies, Dobb presented evidence which
tended to bring into question the trade factor which Sweezy
was to later offer as the primary reason for the
dissolution of feudalism. If trade truely did trigger the
dissolution of feudalism, why did the diminishing of
traditional labor services in favor of rural wage labor
take place first in the southeast of England rather than in
the proximity of London? Why did substantial trade in other
places and other times fail to demolish feudal and other
non-free forms of labor organization? On the latter, Dobb
cites: the Baltic states, Poland, Bohemia, Hungary, at the
end of the fifteenth century; Greek colonies in the second
and third centuries A.D.; and many Russian cities at
various times (Dobb, 1963: 39-42).

     In Studies, there is no mistaking Dobb's position that
feudalism crumbled from within the agricultural setting of
the "natural economy." However, it is in his subsequent
correspondance published in Science and Society that his
position is most clear: "the disintegration of Feudalism
(and hence its final and declining stage) came . . . as a
result of the revolt of the petty producers against feudal
exploitation" (Dobb, 1978b: 100). This observation is of
manifold importance to the present study.

Urban Class Formation

In addition to labor shortages and migration, another
important manifestation of the troubles within the feudal
organization of the labor process was the appearence within
certain towns of a specfically urban class formation: the
addition of free petty commodity producers to the peasantry
and gentry living there.

Essentially three social classes competed within urban
England from the fourteenth to the eighteenth centuries.
The first, the feudal ruling class, was the urban
counterpart to--if not one and the same as--the lay
landlords and others within the traditional rural feudal
system. The second urban class, the merchants, according
to Pirenne (1952: 122ff) descended from the itinerant
traders of the early middle ages. The success of the
itinerant merchants was based upon their abilities to
engage in long distance trade: "To get high prices it was
necessary to seek afar the products which were there found
in abundance, in order to be able to resell them later at a
profit in places where their rarity increased their value."
Moreover, to neatly summarize the position Sweezy was to
later take up: "It was . . . trade over long distances,
that was characteristic of the economic revival of the
middle ages" (Pirenne, 1952: 122). The third class I

characterize as the class of petty commodity producers. Both the petty commodity producers and the merchant class had origins in the peasantry, the historically earlier defectors from agrarian occupations probably became merchants, the later more likely artisan petty producers. The merchants were more likely to have had inter-urban network ties which facilitated their class position and growing economic hegemony in the cities. The petty producers likely had rural-urban networks upon which their subsistence base rested. However, unlike the feudal ruling class, which had a dual basis of existence (both urban and rural), the merchants and the artisans who came to wield power were primarily urban.

Notwithstanding the importance of the urban social classes, I am less inclined to look first toward cities (following Sweezy) or primarily toward rural conditions (following Dobb)--or even to these areas as concepts--for the key to understanding the transition to capitalism and the development of labor migration. For example, events leading to the English Revolution suggest that it was the contradictory class practices within the ruling feudal class at the national level which must be exposed. In this, the rural and urban places simply served as the sites of the contradictory practices. The urban class conflict, which derived to a significant degree from the national ruling-class practices, could be said to be responsible for the development of the bourgeosie and the subsequent installation of most industry in the cities.

Migration plays an important role in this period. To begin with, by the fourteenth and fifteenth centuries, the rural gentry had come to claim residence--to a significant degree--in the towns as well as the manors, in France as well as England. This probably reduced the landlords' abilities to exercise control over the peasant work force and thus must have further contributed to the dissolution of Western European serfdom. While at least in the countryside the gentry could occupy itself with overseeing production by the peasants and thus have some role in the process of production, the division of labor in the cities was such that leisure and urban administration were the gentry's main activities. These two activities of the urban gentry had, by the sixteenth century, become obligatory and indeed burdensome to the point that the urban gentry, "the more substantial citizens," began removing themselves from the larger towns (Phythian-Adams, 1978: 174ff). Quite simply, the costs of urban ceremony, pagentry, and office-holding came to exceed any benefit gained by such practices. As petty commodity production increased, the costs of feudal pagentry came to be passed on to the guilds of petty commodity craft producers. This situation helped to precipitate the return migration of artisans, from city to countryside, which further altered the political economy of the cities.

While the national population may have recovered in numbers and growth rate by the mid-sixteenth century (Gregg, 1976: 199), the recovery could not have been evenly distributed as a number of towns underwent long term declines (Phythian-Adams, 1978: 178). This tendency toward decline and the crisis it ultmately contributed to was met by legislation in the 1550s designed to restrict retail trade to the urban centers. Phythtian-Adams (1978: 179) citing the Records of the City of Norwich explains: "At Norwich it emerges that, before 1554, people had been coming to the city for just long enough to qualify as freemen, and then, before they came liable to urban charges, were departing thence--but now enfranchised to sell their presumably manufactured products in Norwich markets." The cost of feudal ceremony is believed to have reverberated through urban society fostering free merchants and producers unattached to the city and (presumably) accumulating capital in modest amounts. This class shift in economic power, now beyond the control of the feudal state, was one leg upon which the English Civil War, a century later, stood.

The rerustification of the gentry set the stage for
the stratification of the merchant class into two elements:
the urban mercantilists (merchants engaged in long-distance
trade) and the petite bourgeois free merchants (fused with
the petty producers). But the feudalists' decisive
intervention into population redistribution which
contributed to the development of capitalism was the
enclosure movement and the displacement of peasants to the
towns.

Summary

In this chapter, I have demonstrated the processes by
which the enclosure movement and state intervention
directly impacted upon the population structure and the
process of migration in early modern England. State
intervention acted to restrain population movement and
contributed to national repopulation in that the rural rate
of natural increase was greater than the urban. However,
the enclosure movement and changes in the urban class
structure encouraged growth in urban areas at the expense
of national repopulation. This redistribution of
population from the rural areas to the cities, and the
accompanying changes in the urban class structure,
demonstrate the means by which, state intervention
notwithstanding, population homeostasis was established at
a lower level as suggested in hypothesis three.

For a long period, the state and the enclosers worked counter to one another on the enclosure issue though the state eventually came to embrace enclosure as the proto-bourgeois agents within the feudal political hierarchy gained the upper hand in Parliament on the eve of the English Civil War. While the cause of the English Civil War cannot be reduced to struggles over enclosure, I have demonstrated how political and demographic processes associated with enclosure contributed to the fundamental restructuring of English society. This restructuring was signalled by the Civil War, the first successful bourgeois revolution.

Capitalism could not have developed as it did without the surplus population unencumbered by bond to lord or land and concentrated within close enough proximity to provide the work force for industrial production. Nor could capitalism have developed without the concentration in cities of wealth and those who controlled it. But the concentration of wealth and its owners in cities was not unique to early modern England. Cities, we know, were the loci of wealth and power in a wide range of pre-capitalist settings. What was important about concentrations of wealth and cities in England was the class formation which took place. The city, however, was not the decisive factor, it was merely a catalyist. The decisive factor was the process of class struggles.

The class struggle is so important that in the next chapter, I depart temporarily from the general homeostatic approach to that of a class analysis. The historical materialist method demands that class relations be revealed to fully demonstrate the social processes associated with migration. I will subsequently demonstrate that the social structural changes brought about by the class struggles of early modern England established a new population homeostasis allowing, if not requiring, far greater numbers than was characteristic of the post-plague era.

CHAPTER VII

SOCIAL CLASS IN ENGLAND AT THE EVE

OF THE BOURGEOIS EPOCH

The English class system was (and still is) extremely complex and does not easily lend itself to the summary treatment which follows. This is in large part because of the Civil War and its aftermath and the multiple dimensions of class in England in the period of which I write. Not only are classes and class fractions found connected with both the expiring feudal mode of production and the emergent capitalist mode, but above all, this transition period was visited with the petty commodity mode of production associated with the rise of the middle classes. Moreover, one's place within the system of production was not the only criterion of class. One's lineage, one's residence, one's lifestyle, one's income, one's politico-legal status, even one's physical appearance--all interacted to define one's place within society and within the various systems of production. For this reason, I elect to focus upon the structural elements of class formation connecting the framework of the analysis to society mainly in the context of population and occupation.

No hypotheses are specifically addressed in this chapter.
Chapter seven is intended to serve as a dividing point
between the analysis of migration in what is essentially
the period of feudal decline (chapters five and six) and
the period of capitalist development (chapters eight
through eleven). The class analysis proposed here is
intended to highlight the social structural transformation
from the feudal mode of productiom to the capitalist mode
of production in England.

The Ruling Class

The traditional feudal ruling class had its base in
the ownership of land and the control of serf labor. The
crown personified the feudal ruling class even beyond the
end of feudalism. The lay or ecclesiastical status, the
hierarchial position within the feudal vassalage system,
the ideological means of controlling the peasant
producers--all these and more--were important then, but
shed little light upon the class structure. The essential
structural elements I am interested in concern the
ownership and control of labor power and the means of
production. The feudal ruling class--especially before the
reformation when the Catholic church was included--owned
the very greatest part of the land and controlled
substantial numbers of serf laborers. This ruling class
retained effective control of the English state until

Charles I found it necessary to summon the Long Parliament
in 1660 whereby the bourgeois-controlled Parliament, in the
course of the Civil War, put an end to feudal power. This
represented the finale in the long decline in the economic
foundations of feudal power. The crown's power and the
feudal economy had diminished through the ages both in
relation to feudalism's heyday before the Magna Charta and
in relation to the emergent merchant and petty producer
classes which took control of the state apparatus from the
middle of the seventeenth century.

Two important population factors contributed to the
demise of the feudal ruling class: residence and
reproductivity. I have already noted the expenditures on
ceremony and administration required of members of the
ruling class with urban residency. The Reformation not only
shifted the balance of power in Parliament from the clergy
to the lay peers but also signalled the significant
diminution of ceremonial (unproductive) consumption of the
social surplus within the urban political economy. These
changes probably came too late to relieve the aristocracy
from the adverse impact of the financial burdens of
pageantry, as they learned to pass the obligation off to
the middle-class guilds of merchants and petty producers.
The middle classes, however, were able to prosper in the
post-sixteenth century towns leaving the core elements of

the feudal ruling class with their manorial rather than
urban political economy.

Where the traditional feudal class benefitted,
paradoxically, was in its high reproductivity. With the
system of primogeniture, the increasing rate of natural
increase within the aristocratic population meant that
either the feudal system must itself be expanded or some
offspring must be socially mobile out of the feudal ruling
class. In the early period of population increase (the
eleventh through the thirteenth centuries), feudal
production was expanded by colonization and settlement. In
the post-recovery period of population growth, from the
sixteenth century on, the opportunities to expand feudal
production were severely limited. Some younger sons of
peers may have acquired ecclesiastical lands after the
Reformation, but most entered into skilled crafts or became
merchants. Thus, the untitled among the higher order gentry
were articulated with the rising middle classes.

The Middle Class

By the beginning of the sixteenth century there had
emerged at least three distinct fractions of the "middle
class." The merchants were urban-based and connected with
both long-distance and local trade. The petty producers of
commodities such as textiles, tools, or clothing were

either urban or rural based. The genuinely rural middle
class--the yeoman farmers, rich peasants, well-to-do
tenants--were agriculturalists or pastoralists producing
either food or wool for consumption or further processing
into durable commodities. Let me discuss each fraction in
turn.

The Merchant Fraction

The leading commercial stratum, the merchants involved
in long-distance trade, effected a double articulation with
the state. On the one hand, as I have mentioned, members of
the feudal ruling class, often with the highest of
connections, entered into trade. A complimentary
countermove to this was the practice of wealthy merchants
purchasing estates and titles--the latter from the crown
which seems to have been in perennial need of money. With
regard to population and occupation, the richer,
international trading stratum of merchants came to be
indistinguishable in its place within the economy from the
merchant stratum of the aristocracy. On the other hand,
this class of international merchants came to be
articulated with the state at another level of analysis
(from about the middle of the sixteenth century) with the
emergence of mercantilist ideology and the system of
colonialism this engendered. The plunder and enslavement of

the indiginous peoples of Africa, Asia, and the Americas
gave "colonization" a new meaning. These international
merchants, deriving their superprofits increasingly from
"trade" with the colonies, developed the basic elements of
modern capitalist finance and exchange. The impact of this
class can hardly be underestimated.

Local merchant "middlemen" or middle agents were at a
distinct disadvantage to their London counterparts who were
engaged primarily in international trade. Capital for
provincial trade was scarce and expensive. The consistent
profits of the mercantilists (with losses in international
trade insured by underwriters in London) escaped the
townsmerchants. It is my position that the importance of
cities to capitalist development did not emerge to the
front until the mercantilist period--in contrast to Sweezy
and Pirenne. Given the mercantilists' need for
concentration of markets and capital, they would
necessarily have invented cities, if cities had not already
existed. Indeed, in the peripheral areas from Capetown to
the "Old Whore on the Mekong," Third World cities are
today, what they are, largely because of the intrusion of
colonialism (and this is no less true of the suffering the
Old Whore, Phnom Penh, has undergone in recent years.)

Local petty merchants, therefore, operated at a
distinct disadvantage to the London-based mercantilists.

Not only that, but before the industrial revolution with its proliferation of cheap consumer goods, the local retail trade was also in competition with the local petty producers who often sold directly to the consumer. Even the middle agents who purchased raw materials from the sources, like the staplers who traded in wool (as opposed to cloth), were not assured of reasonable economic security until the domestic industrial economy emerged--for the staplers, the English textile industry had to reach such a level that they no longer needed to meet one of the twice yearly shippings to Calais for textile production in Europe. The small merchant staplers, however, were viable only as long as the production of cloth remained small-scale with the staplers' petty producer customers making modest weekly purchases. As the scale of production in the textile industry increased with the industrial revolution, the middle merchant wool broker came to be obsolete as large clothiers delt more directly with the growers. Along with the wool trade which increasingly centered upon London, even inter-regional trade in such goods as coal, grain, livestock, and cloth, were transshipped through London.

Apart from the dimensions of internal trade just mentioned, much of the local trade continued to be carried on by very small operators in the town fairs and markets. Such practices were, in the end, not viable. The merchant middle class stratum which gained hegemony before the industrial revolution was the mercantilist.

In all likelihood, the population growth within the urban-based merchant middle class was easily absorbed by occupations within that class. The same could probably be said about the urban petty producers, too. The growth of trade and craft occupations in London and other major urban centers could not be matched by the urban rate of natural increase in population. Even before the industrial revolution, there was an economic draw upon the towns and villages by the cities. Migration continued and London grew. London grew as both the center of trade and (later) the center of industry.

The Industrial Fraction

Before London became the center of industrial production in the eighteenth century, petty commodity production was probably not qualitatively different from that in other towns, the scale of production being dependent upon the size of the local market. Shoemakers, tailors, brewers--many consumer goods producers remained small-scale and ubiquitous. It was the extraction and processing of localized raw materials in the sixteenth, seventeenth, and early eighteenth centuries which fed class formation outside the cloth industry. With a few exceptions, the production remained essentially petty commodity/petty bourgeois. Let me review these industrial developments.

Salt, glass, pottery, bricks, and paper were among the more important of the minor industries which emerged in the sixteenth and seventeenth centuries. Salt, glass, and paper in particular were import substitutes and generally of lower quality (and with salt in particular much more expensive to manufacture) than similar products imported from the continent. Part of this was due to inferior English technology and part due to enviromental factors. In such industries, a certain degree of wage labor was found as an appendage to the petty commodity mode of their production. For example, Sir W. Brerton's observations of 1634-35 indicated that a salt manufacturer realized a yearly profit about four times the size of the total wages paid (Jack, 1977: 172). Skilled glass workers, according to Jack (1977: 91), had such high wages once imported techniques had been adopted that a principal worker earning eighteen shillings in a day (about twice to three times the usual daily wage) could live as a gentleman. The profit of one glass maker cited (Jack 1977: 172-73) was only about two and one-half times the wages paid in fairly small-scale production units. Wage levels were likely to have fallen as scales of production increased; enterprises employing a thousand workers were not unknown as of the mid-seventeenth century according to Hill (1969: 172). Of the petty commodity industries producing consumer goods, leather was possibly second in importance to cloth (Jack, 1977: 108ff). Leather production was one of the best examples of petty commodity production in that it required relatively high capital inputs (owing to the length of time the tanning process took and the ground space required) and small labor inputs. Leather was used mainly for clothing and as an instrument of production, for example in the manufacture of horses' collars. Leather products, however, did not readily lend themselves to mass production in part due to the increasing availibility of substitutes like cloth and because some applications required custom fitting for most efficient use.

The role of the cloth industry in the development of the British industrial economy is too well-known to require special attention here. We need only note the class character of its production on the eve of the industrial revolution and its relationship to migration. Concomitant with the dissolution of the staplers guild, the clothiers came to control the labor process from the purchase of fleece to the sale of finished cloth. One of the key productive roles the clothiers played was in the dyeing of the material--this the clothiers themselves did. Spinning

and weaving was usually put out to specialists in those
respective occupations though some looms may have been
owned by clothiers. A single loom could employ some forty
people and minor technical improvements to the looms were
brought by Protestant refugees from the continent (Jack,
1977: 101-105). But the sixteenth century was the last to
see the dominance of English broadcloths among textile
exports. The following century saw the overtaking of these
heavy cloths by the "new draperies," lighter in weight and
sometimes made of silk, cotten, or linen and thus more
suitable for consumption in warmer climates. The importance
of this innovation introduced by the Flemings is that the
new draperies were more suitable to large-scale,
capitalized production (Hill, 1969: 86-87, 172;
Wallerstein, 1974: 277, 279 n. 264). In summary, the
textile industry's technology and markets were well-suited
to mass industrial production in the opening decades of the
capitalist mode of production. What the industry needed
above all, and what it received through urbanization, was a
large, cheap labor force.

The extractive industries--viz. coal and iron
mining--were material requisites of capitalist
industrialization. Not only were they necessary for
industrial production in other sectors, but their own
extraction and processing utilized labor processes which

were readily adaptable to capitalist production. Writing

about the early seventeenth century, Christopher Hill

(1969: 59) observes that

> During this period a proletariat began to be
> differentiated from the rest of society organized
> in guilds and manors. Industrial specialization,
> especially in mining, produced workmen who were
> dirtier than their fellows; being less well fed
> their teeth tended to decay early, their children
> to be deformed by rickets.

Iron and coal were the leading proto-capitalist mining

industries. Other minerals mined, especially copper and

lead, were on smaller scales with lead in particular mined

by "free minors", essentially petty bourgeois workers as in

a gold rush. Attempts to mine alum (an important ingredient

in dyes and relatively scarce in England) under a seeming

state capitalist organization became a financial debacle in

the first decade of the seventeenth century. However, one

important ingredient of the mining industry in general was

the importation of skilled labor from the continent,

especially Germany. Jack (1977: 73) goes so far as to

suggest that in the mid-sixteenth century, with iron

smelting, "what was probably most significant of all, the

availibility of men skilled in the new techniques was even

more limited than capital."[28]

---

[28] Jack (1977: 67-85) surveys the extractive
industries of the sixteenth and seventeenth centuries.

The shipbuilding industry was extremely important to England's emergence as the world power. While the greatest importance of shipbuilding lay in the use of its product in international trade (and warfare, the two not always being distinguishable), the industry also helped engender the proletarianization of the work force. The employers in the shipbuilding industry, however, would seem to have been the mercantilists and other shipowners. While the organization of production was along capitalist or quasi-capitalist lines, the ownership of the means of production was not in the hands of a capitalist class (strictly defined) but rather the mercantilist class (Jack, 1977: 99-101). The other main industry which harvested the high seas, fishing, was even more petty-bourgeois oriented. Sailors were not paid wages, but they shared with the officers and master one-third of the value of the catch. A second third went to the owner and the final third to the victualler (Jack, 1977: 93-97, 174-181)

The Rural Fraction

The question of the rural fraction of the middle class--yeoman farmers, rich peasants, lesser gentry, well-to-do tenants--is more clouded. They were essentially petty bourgeois agriculturalists or pastoralists who controlled the means of production either by ownership or tenancy. Moreover, their control over labor was not based upon traditional feudal dues. They would be distinguished structurally from landlords and other feudalists on the one hand, and from the rural proletarians and vagabonds who, on the other hand, did not possess sufficient land to earn their means of subsistence. Measured in centuries, The free landed peasantry, as a middle class was a relative late-comer, thouge its predecessor pre-dated feudalism. At the height of the feudal period, the countryside was dominated by the landlord aristocracy with both free and unfree peasants providing labor. As the feudal relations of production broke down, a "middle peasantry" emerged--tenants and copyholders with no claim upon their labor time held by the landlord class. These yeoman farmers, lesser gentry, and retirees from urban life came to form the rural middle class.

As intimated above, several key characteristics distinguished the rural middle class from the traditional feudal lords and the peasant-proletariat. The middle-class farmers engaged in actual productive labor and/or capitalist estate management. The latter in particular implied their use of wage labor and their acquision of land to increase the scale of production. From working, petty-producing peasants, this middle-class fraction tended to stratify into either capitalist farmers or subsistence

farmers, the latter eventually becoming landless laborers.
Unlike the poor peasants who operated at the subsistence
level or less, the capitalist farmers increasingly produced
for the growing markets--both the urban food market and the
corn and wool export markets. This rural middle class was
most likely to utilize new techniques and technologies of
production: horses replaced oxen; enclosure of both arable
and pasture land; increased use of manure; etc. to increase
productivity. By the eve of the industrial revolution, the
most important stratum of the rural middle class--if one
could still call it middle class--was the capitalist
farmer, having been joined in no small part by the former
feudal landlords after the final dissolution of feudal
tenures in the seventeenth century.

According to Hill (1969: 61), "Historians are coming
more and more to agree that capital accumulated in
agriculture, often in the form of small savings, may in the
long run have been more important than the contribution of
trade and industry." It was this fraction of the middle
class: especially the articulation of the landlord
aristocrats freed from their obligations to the crown after
1646 (see Hill, 1969: 146-54) with wealthy commoners
engaging in capitalist estate management, that was the
capital accumulating class which caught Hill's attention.
The general development of the market economy, enclosures,

and rack-renting tended to eliminate the poorer stratum of the rural middle class: the copyholders and tenants with small holdings and insecure tenure.

The Landless Poor

The general direction of class formation and the specific economic and agricultural factors discussed in this chapter contributed to the emergence of a mass of landless peasants, vagabonds, and poor urban in-migrants. The landless peasantry formed the work force utilized by the capitalist farmers and in mining and other heavy industries. As a class, the landless peasantry probably more closely resembled the proletariat (albeit of a rural variety) than the capitalist farmers or mercantilists did a truely capitalist class. But the work available to the rural proletariat was grossly inadequate considering the numbers of dispossessed peasants. Eventually, these peasants were to become the city poor of whom Dickens has written. But in the interlude between peasantry and urban proletarian, many became vagabonds or beggars.

There was nothing new about vagabondism. Itinerant peasants were evident throughout the middle ages, these wayfarers being both lay (herbalists, charatans, minstrels, juglers, messengers, peddlers, outlaws, workers, etc.) and religious (preachers, friars, pardoners, and pilgrams)

according to Jusserand (1889). For the most part, these
itinerants of the medieval period came to form the merchant
and petty-producing middle classes. In the last centuries
before the industrial revolution, however, when the
population was growing and the agricultural lands were
being enclosed, a great many peasants were reduced to
beggary, vagabondage, and the unemployed. What is important
to note at this point is the de classe nature of these
former serfs, proto-proletarians. This great mass of poor
was probably the largest social issue of the early modern
period. Those peasants who were unable to find agricultural
employment, or worse still, employment in the mines, were
too often forced to enter their children into workhouses
(usually to die within a short time), and themselves into
equally insufferable institutions designed for the poor.
The modern capitalist factory had its origins in both the
Dickensian England of the poor and the middle-class
workshops. One inference from of this study is that in
each conjuncture of capitalist development, it is the poor
and de classe social strata (whether they be Irish peasants
or Vietnamese compradores) of societies undergoing
fundamental structural changes that fuel the engines of the
capitalist labor process. And unlike the distribution of
fossil fuels, it does make economic sense for the
capitalist to send human coals to Newcastle.

Class Struggles

The key to following the class struggles of early
modern England is to acknowledge the emergence of a modern
bourgeoisie from the middle class fractions which grew out
of the decline of feudalism. The bourgeoisie has its roots
in both the commercial middle class, especially the
mercantilists, and the sections of the feudal aristocracy
which had managed to breed itself off the land.

The new bourgeoisie had a Calvinist orientation: this
represented the ascendency of Protestantism over feudal
Catholicism. Accompanied by Calvinism, the bourgeoisie
could join the scientific rebellion against the Catholic
church. But perhaps most important, as Engels put it, as
cited in Hill (1948: 153):

> Calvin's creed was one fit for the boldest of
> the bourgeoisie of his time. His doctrine of
> predestination was the religious expression of
> the fact that in the commercial world of
> competition success or failure does not depend
> upon a man's activity or cleverness but upon
> circumstances uncontrollable by him. . . .
> Calvin's church constitution was thoroughly
> democratic and republican; and when the kingdom
> of God was republicanized, could the kingdoms of
> this world remain subject to monarchs, bishops
> and lords?

Bourgeois property relations stand at the heart of the
class conflicts of early modern England. No longer could
feudal property based upon land and serfs prevail. Private
property based upon the commoditization of both land and

labor--and the world of commerce which derived from private property--increasingly came to dominate the English economy.

The political hegemoney of the bourgeoisie was somewhat slower in coming. The Reformation had strengthened the property basis of the secular landowners at the expense of the church and had weakened the ideological basis of feudalism by the defeat of the Catholic church. But as Marx suggested, this was only the first step toward bourgeois power: "Before secular feudalism could be successfully attacked in each country and in detail, . . . [the Catholic church,] its spiritual central organization, had to be destroyed" (cited in Hill, 1948: 152). The crown remained feudalistic throughout the Tudor and Stuart regimes.

The last of the Stuart kings, James I and Charles I, came into increased conflict with the bourgeois-dominated Parliament. This Parliament, representing English merchants, peers, and gentlemen, resisted the autocratic behavior of James I and Charles I. Parliament's resistence to the king was based upon the Magna Charta and the rule of law. When Parliament issued it's 1628 Petition of Right which cited the legal limitations upon the king, Charles I dismissed Parliament and ruled for eleven years before again summoning Parliament. In this period, the king

raised funds illegally and attempted to establish the
Church of England in Scotland. When the Scots revolted,
the English soldiers called up by Charles mutinied forcing
Charles to call upon Parliament for financial support.
Parliament, now representing the wealthiest class, the
bourgeoisie, refused.

The Civil War which resulted from the
king-Parliamentary conflict saw Oliver Cromwell raise an
army of diverse class origins, reflecting the diversity of
opposition to the king. The peasantry and the rural middle
class supported Cromwell and the London bourgeoisie. The
beheading of Charles I in 1649 ushered in a republican
period in which England quickly established itself as a
major military power at sea and a protagonist of European
royalty. With the death of Cromwell, however, the radical
elements suffered a serious set-back as Charles II was
installed on the throne in 1660. According to Professor
Hill (1948: 150-151):

> The restoration of 1660 was inspired by the
> fear of popular democracy felt by the solid
> merchants and the country gentry who had acquired
> all they wanted from the revolution. Charles II
> was prepared to accept the rule of the
> bourgeoisie in fact, where Charles I had refused:
> so the monarchy, the House of Lords and the
> Church of England were restored and the
> revolutionary army disbanded. The compromise of
> 1660 swung too far to the right: although
> Charles II was prudent, James II took seriously
> the fiction that he was King by the grace of God.
> The "Revolution" of 1688 readjusted the balance
> and made the rule of the bourgeoisie and
> capitalist landlords explicit[.] . . .

Henceforth the compromise between big
bourgeoisie and landlords ruled England until the
balance was shifted in 1832 to admit the
industrial bourgeoisie to a share in power.

Briefly then, by a combination of the force of numbers

and of economic power, the bourgeoisie was able to

establish its own hegemony within the state apparatus.

Demographic factors, not the least of which which was

migration, contributed to the economic and political

conditions which were behind the bourgeoisie's success.   A

major theme of this thesis is that the capitalist system,

itself, contributes to the propensity of peoples to

migrate.   I shall explore this theme in the following

chapters.

CHAPTER VIII

POPULATION AND THE ANTECEDENTS OF THE SEVENTEENTH
CENTURY CRISIS

The previous chapter ended with a short discussion of
the seventeenth century class struggles in England which
resulted in the acquisition of state power by the
bourgeoisie. While England was the only seventeenth
century country which saw the gaining of power by a
national bourgeoisie capable of fostering capitalist
production, European monarchs saw a series of insurrections
and other challenges to authority and the class basis of
feudal power. The purpose of this and the following
chapter is to develop and explore the thesis that the
bourgeois epoch which was ushered in during the seventeenth
century marked a major turning point in migration history.
The structural basis of this conjuncture is inextricably
bound to the political economy of the European crisis. The
present chapter addresses selected cultural, environmental,
economic, and demographic antecedents of the seventeenth
century crisis. The next chapter analyses the impact upon
international migration of a structural discord within the

European economy as it passed through the seventeenth century crisis period and entered the industrial revolution.

From Iberia to Ireland, France to the Ukraine, Eastern and Western Europe saw what Hobsbawm (1954a: 37) was to characterize as the seventeenth century of "social revolt." We are interested in the reasons for this strife-torn century and in its ultimate impact because it is believed that demographic factors--particularly migration--figured prominantly in both its causes and effects. Among the most important demographic factors which may be said to have contributed to the general crisis of the seventeenth century was the recovery of the population from the series of plagues and famines which had depopulated Europe from the fourteenth century onward.

Hypothesis Four

Cultural practices maintained population homeostasis at the lower, post-crisis level.

Discussion: Cultural Practices

Specifically, I argue that changes in the normative age of marriage and in household composition patterns helped to constrain the regrowth of population by constraining fertility while also contributing to the

mobility of the population. In a society where relatively
few illegitimate births take place, as was the situation in
England in the pre-industrial period (Chambers, 1972: 44),
the usual age at first marriage is an important fertility
limiter. Household composition, or the number of
generations residing within the household, is related to
marriage norms but may also have important affects upon
population, economy, and society. The combination of
conditions which encourage fertility will contribute to the
tendency toward population growth. Following the
population crisis of the fourteenth century, stagnation set
in with replacement of the numbers lost delayed a number of
generations. It is believed that male postponement of
marriage for economic reasons and the remarriage of widows
of means near the end of their fecund period tended to
restrict the level of fertility needed to replace the lost
population numbers. The intergenerational composition of
households also restrained fertility but encouraged
migration. Mortality patterns, marriage practices, and
household composition in the fifteenth century may have
encouraged migration both of couples (to communities where
land was available or work to be had) and of individuals
(for economic and marriage opportunities). The net impact,
within the overall environmental and socio-economic
setting, was a stagnation in population growth with the

size of the population stabilized well below that which
immediately preceded the plagues of the fourteenth century.
From about the beginning of the sixteenth century and
onwards, population growth re-emerged, fuelled by social
and economic changes which stimulated both migration and
fertility. This increased population, in turn, stimulated
economic growth.

The impact of the church upon the family must be
noted.[29] As early as the thirteenth century,
ecclesiastical control over marriage customs had come into
conflict with, and began to override, feudal custom. This
tended to reduce the political hold the manorial lords had
upon their serfs: the ability to wed without the consent
of the lord(s) and the acquisition of the right to make
wills (thus gaining control over property), contributed
toward the gradual erosion of the unfree conditions of the
enserfed peasantry, even before the population
retrogression.

It is not clear at what point the two-generation
family came to predominate over the extended family though
the findings Chambers (1972: 35ff) cites indicate that the
nuclear family was evident, if not the norm, before the

---

[29] Chambers (1972: 41-42) suggests that Christian
asceticism may have acted to increase the age of first
marriage, thus reducing fertility where women entered
into marriage at a later age.

fourteenth century. The importance of this is that where primogeniture predominated, second and later sons were left landless and thus faced with considerable financial uncertainty--a condition which tended to delay or preclude marriage and/or encourage emigration to other areas or the cities where an apprenticeship might be had. The contradictory impact of this situation was, on the one hand, a restraint upon rapid population growth and thus the massive labor surplus needed to fuel the industrial revolution; while on the other hand, legal and customary barriers against migration increasingly yielded to the reality of landlessness created both by these demographic and cultural factors and by the enclosure of agricultural lands.

The result of enclosures, two-generation households, and inheritance patterns--which tended to restrain population growth through much of the fifteenth century--was increased landlessness and peasant mobility. As feudalism dissolved in the centuries between the fourteenth and the industrial revolution, landless peasants increasingly tended to establish themselves in the cities.

Hypothesis Five

Overseas colonial emigration and rural depopulation
contributed to the sixteenth century price revolution.

Discussion: Sixteenth Century Price Revolution

On the one hand, the net out-migration from the
European system in the early colonial period was countered
economically by a net importation of specie. This increase
in the total quantity of gold and silver in Europe, I would
argue, contributed to the price revolution. On the other
hand, demand-pull inflation which originated in the
agricultural sector of late feudal society was itself the
result of the regrowth of the rural population, once the
period of population stagnation had passed.

The seventeenth century crisis was preceded by about a
century of European price inflation of unprecedented
proportions. The inflation began between about 1475 and
1510 depending upon what part of Europe one considers and
which authority one consults (see, for example, Braudel,
1967: 401ff; Usher, 1931: 110; or Hamilton, 1929:
350-354).

The general course of the sixteenth century
inflationary period in England is demonstrated by Figure 1,
Eurpean wheat prices, 1450-1649. According to Braudel
(1967: 407-416) the price of wheat is representative of

food prices in general. R.B. Outhwaite (1969), in a review
of the literature on the economy of the sixteenth century,
has broadly categorized the theoretical attempts to explain
the inflation as either "monetary" (1969:   23-36) or "real
or physical" (1969:   37-47). Each type of explanation has
direct or indirect demographic implications.

The monetary argument was the one most frequently
found in Outhwaite's perusal of the writings of
contemporaries though they seem to have been less aware of
the secular trend, commenting upon the inflation during
those periods when it was most rapid.   The causes cited
then, and still the mainstay of the monetary argument, were
(1) the debasements of national currencies which took place
in many countries on a number of occasions and (2) the
influx of treasure from the Americas through Spain.

Monetary explanations found a theoretical basis in the
quantity theory of money which argues that value is
inversely proportional to the quantity of money in
circulation.   The "real" explanations of inflation, which
probably have more followers now, focus upon population
growth trends, high governmental war expenditures, and the
disaggregated price inflation differentials.   On the latter
point, rent and agricultural prices are said to have risen
more rapidly than industrial prices and wages.   While I
lean more heavily toward the real of explanation, I must

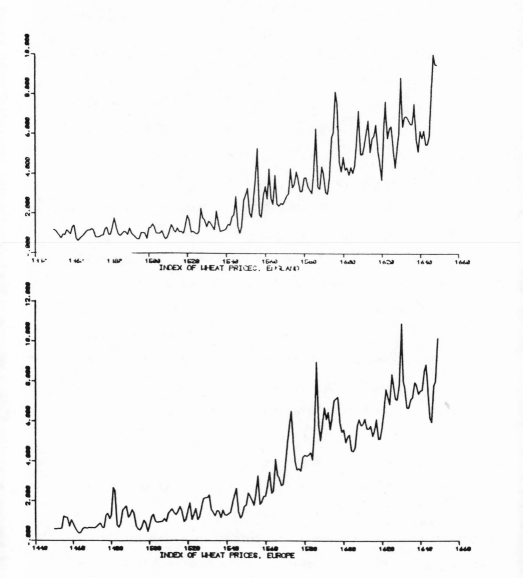

FIGURE 1: Wheat Price Index, England and Western Euro⟨pe⟩
(1450-99=1.00)
Source: Bowden, 1967: 851-55

also admit the possibility that the importion of gold and silver from the Americas may have contributed to the general rate of inflation. But perhaps even more important than admitting to multiple causality (Outhwaite, 1969: 42, cautions against "making population pressure do all the work which was formerly undertaken by Spanish treasure"), is recognizing the uneven development of economic forces of primitive accumulation. I argue that the structural differences between the Iberian and English economies--in particular--must be explored alongside their demographic histories in order to gain some understanding of the inflationary period and its subsequent crisis.

Monetary Explanations

Let me examine the monetary argument first. To begin with, I find less theoretical basis for the hypothesis that debasement of currency was a major cause of inflation as opposed to one which finds devaluation an attendant condition--rather than a cause--of inflation. If debasement were a bonafide major causal explanation, it presupposes its own unexplained political cause, one which was supra-national in nature. It makes much more sense to see debasement (and whatever impact it may have had upon inflation) as the European states' main means of coping with existing inflation. Hammarstrom (1957: 152-154) does not find debasement an important factor in the price revolution. She does, however, note that in both the sixteenth century and the middle ages there were class-based antagonisms surrounding debasement in several countries. The "trading sections of the population" pressured the government to mint more coinage even if it meant a debasement while the "landowners who had fixed incomes from the rents, vigorously opposed the debasement of the coinage" (1957: 154, note deleted).

On the question of the importation of Spanish-American silver especially, but also gold, the monetary argument may have more strength. Following the view most often associated with Hamilton (1977), Andre Gunder Frank (1978: 50-51) argues that regardless of the seeming appearance of inflation prior to the influx of precious metals (see Usher, 1931: 110 or Braudel, 1967: 401ff), the American bullion was at least partially responsible for the inflation and the lowering of real wages which ensued. And a point which cannot be ignored is that migration and colonization led by the Iberian powers was initiated first in the quest for treasure.

Real Explanations

The lowering of real wages (see Figure 2) also resulted from the differential rates of inflation between food prices and wages (see Braudel, 1967: 419-455). Let me examine the argument which disaggregates the rates of inflation.

While caution must be exercised in placing too much confidence in any data (price, wage, population, etc.) gathered in the centuries before the present,[30] those data which are available suggest very strongly the possiblity that agricultual prices rose more rapidly than industrial. On this point, see Figure 3 which is plotted from indices of the prices of a composite unit of foodstuffs and of a sample of industrial products calculated by E.H. Phelps Brown and Sheila V. Hopkins It seems evident that this was not an isolated phenomenon. Why did this take place?

Brown and Hopkins (1957; 1959), Outhwaite (1969), and Helliener (1967: 24) attribute the inflation to population increase and the disaggregated rates of inflation are in keeping with this explanation. That is, if population (demand for food) increased at a greater rate than did the

---

[30] See Hammarstrom's (1957: 118-120) discussion of some methodological problems involved in working with the time series of price and wage data from this period.

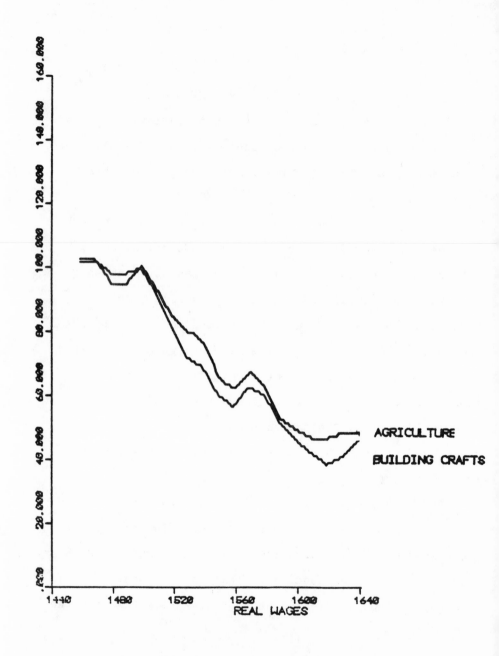

FIGURE 2:   Index of Real Wages, Southern England, 1450-1649
Twenty-year Moving Average
Source: based on Bowden, 1967:   865

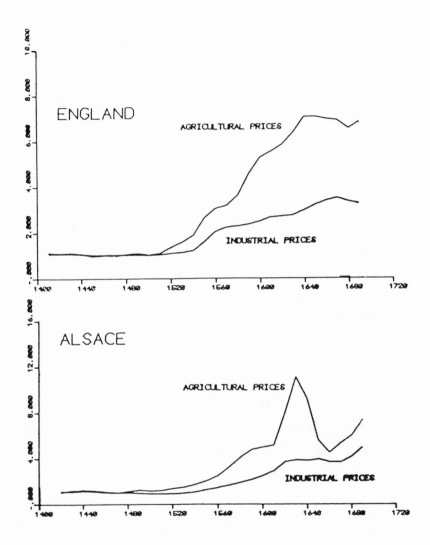

FIGURE 3:   Price Indices of Agricultural and Industrial
            Products: England and Alsace
         Twenty-year Moving Average (1451-75=1.00)
         Source: based on Brown and Hopkins, 1981:   77

production of food stuffs--most European agricultural production still being tied to the archaic feudal mode of production--a case could be made for demand-pull inflation within the agricultural sector. Add to this the enclosure movement in some areas with the transfer of land use from food to wool production and the demand-pull argument may be strengthened. Moreover, the rising rents aided the process of accumulation to the benefit of certain elements within the agrarian economy: (1) those landlords unrestricted by fixed rental contracts and able to rack rents and (2) the "many freeholding peasants . . . , provided they had enough land to feed themsleves even in bad years, a regular surplus for sale, and a good head for business" (Hobsbawm, 1954a: 48, note deleted). As to the industrial sector--textiles, mining, etc.--such production before the industrial revolution remained highly labor intensive. The increasing price of food, felt in the industrial employers' accounts as higher wages, suggests the existence of cost-push inflation in the industrial sector. One main reason for the difference between the foodstuff and industrial product inflation rates was probably associated with the tendency for workers' real wages to fall, as wage labor was a more important factor of production in industry than agriculture in the late feudal period. While workers seem to have registered some wage increases (even in the troubled seventeenth century) the growth of population and the movement of peasants from enclosed estates, plague-stricken communities, etc. likely contributed to a labor surplus. The labor surplus implies the emergence of a relative surplus population.

The sixteenth century European price revolution adversely affected those elements of society with fixed incomes and dependent upon the market for supplies of food (in particular). In general these elements included (1) government, for example, the English government which was restricted in its ability to raise taxes, (2) the landlords with tenants possessing long-term fixed rents at low rates, and (3) wage workers--especially the landless. One might argue that an important contribution to the bourgeois revolution in England was the disadvantageous position the inflation placed upon the crown vis-a-vis the bourgeois Parliament. It might further be argued that the crowns of Europe were themselves to blame, at least in part, for the inflation which drained their treasuries. Some theorists of the "real" school (Hill, 1969: 82-83; Outhwaite, 1969: 43) attribute the inflation in part to preparations for war which also played an important role in the seventeenth century crisis. War carried to the extreme (e.g. the Thirty Years War) was in some places so devastating as to bring on national economic declines (Dobb, 1963: 239), though Hobsbawm (1954a: 38-39) cautions that economic decline also appeared in places which were untouched by war.

To extract the central points from the discussion of inflation developed thus far:

1. Insofar as (and if) American treasure played any role in the sixteenth century inflation, it was clearly connected with colonization and hence with migration.[31]

2. There was a price inflation differential between food and industrial products which suggests demographic factors of causation and has class implications for its effects.

3. The more widely held view at present is that population growth made an important contribution to inflation.

Let me explore the demographic argument in more detail.

---

[31] I should mention here that no less an authority than Schumpeter ridiculed the very idea that the influx of precious metals had anything to do with the sixteenth century price revolution, which itself Schumpeter thought had had its dimensions exagerated by historians. According to Schumpeter, "To reduce the social process of [the period of which we are writing] . . . to monetary processes, bears the stamp of monetary monomania" (1939 I: 233 n. 1).

Homeostasis and the Demographic Transition

There is no doubt but that European population growth returned sometime after the fourteenth century. Just exactly when and at what rate are questions which cannot be answered with any certainty. Nor can we know for sure why population grew--and continued to grow far beyond the peak we believe it reached in the early fourteenth century. And even though the sixteenth century price revolution is now attributed in some part to population growth, we are not completely certain of this, nor do we know for sure what else--if anything--resulted from population growth. Let me attempt to shed some light upon the matters in question.

Hypothesis Six

Environmental factors in the post-crisis period constrained the actual population size to the lower limits of population homeostasis.

Regarding the demographic transition, my hypothesis is that two major environmental factors acted to keep population near the lower limits of the homeostatic carrying capacity. Periodic episodes of high mortality due to pestilence and crop failures acted to constrain population far below its theoretical carrying capacity. This is to be distinguished from the establishment of a lower population homeostasis, per se. Countering this tendency, however, were environmental and socio-economic changes which acted to establish a higher population homeostasis. (The ultimate relief from environmentally-caused mortality allowed the size of the population to rise toward its optimum level.)

Hypothesis Seven

From the time of the price revolution, socio-economic changes contributed to a higher population homeostasis.

A further dimension of the foregoing hypotheses is the hypothesis that in the course of the socio-economic adaptation to the environmental pressure on population, a situation presenting the potential for increase in actual population size could be said to exist, awaiting diminution (especially) of the urban mortality rate. Demographically, this adaptation appeared in the form of high rural fertility coupled with high rates of urbanization (population redistribution from areas of relatively high rates of natural increase to areas of relatively low). In addition, consumption patterns may have been altered. There are important class implications of this socio-economic adaptation which help explain questions of class formation discussed in previous chapters. Changes associated with consumption likely contributed to the restructuring of the urban economy so as to establish the petty commodity mode of production, and most importantly, the class base upon which it rested: a prosperous merchant class and a skilled class of artisan petty producers. The increased agricultural production for market suggests a parallel class development in rural areas.

Hypothesis Eight

Declines in environmentally and economically induced mortality initiated actual population growth.

My final hypothesis regarding the demographic transition concerns the decline in mortality. Concomitant with the eventual passing of the plague (for environmental reasons which are not fully understood), came the economic ability and technical feasibility for merchants and municipalities to store and transport sufficient quantities of grain to relieve the potential of famine, especially in the cities. Population and economic growth so induced, alongside dissolution of rural feudalism and other social changes, are hypothesized as having provided both the surplus population and the capital necessary for the onset of industrial capitalist production.

Discussion

The homeostatic population model suggests that within
a given socio-economic and natural environmental setting,
population would stabilize at some optimum size.
Nondemographic factors--political, environmental,
cultural--may act through the demographic to cause the
population size to deviate from its homeostatic level.
Compensatory changes would then be expected to homeostasis,
such as by the adaptation of economic practices to a new
homeostatic level in equilibrium with population size or by
demographic corrections to the population, returning it to
homeostasis.

In the present discussion, the unit of analysis
utilized is the nation-state applied to the continent of
Europe. The focus is on the alteration of population
homeostasis (through changes in production, consumption,
and politics) in the face of disequilibrium caused in part
by environmentally-induced changes in mortality. This is
an especially useful approach since population growth took
place in most nations of Europe. Of course, there were
regional and local differentials in the rates of growth,
including (at least for a time, such as in Granada)
negative rates of population growth. Four selected trends
illustrating European population growth are demonstrated in
Figure 4 and Figure 5.

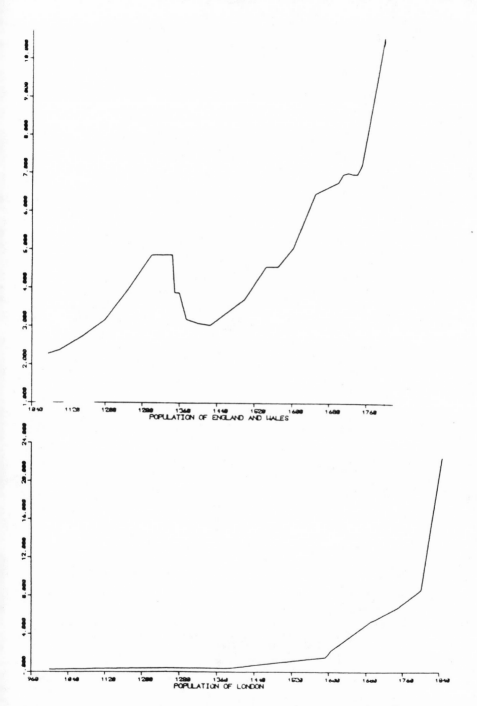

FIGURE 4: Population Trends, United Kingdom
(England and Wales X 1,000,000)
(London X 100,000)
Sources: based on Wrigley, 1969: 78
Chandler and Fox, 1974: 137
Clarkson, 1971: 26

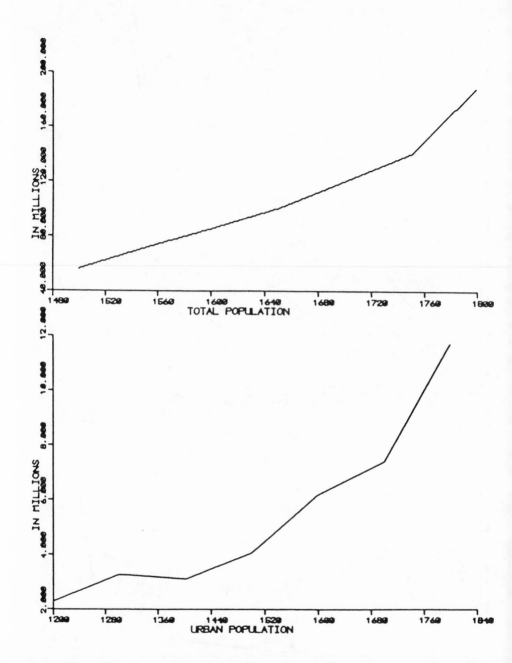

FIGURE 5: Population Trends, Europe
Sources: based on Tilly, 1975: 399
Chandler and Fox, 1974: 12-21

London's recovery from the "Black Death" (see Figure 4), its return to the pre-plague population size, evidently proceeded at a faster rate than did national recovery of England and Wales. This immediate post-plague, urban-led phase of population recovery could be seen from this example as "pull" migration.[32] Urban growth through in-migration proceeded at least in part because many cities eased guild membership to encourage the replacement of the lost urban population. However, it may also have contributed to rural depopulation (Hellenier, 1967: 15). This apparant urban-led recovery should be seen as a phenomenon separate from the later "demographic transition." The European urban and London trends illustrated in Figure 4 and Figure 5 suggest the possibility that London's rapid pre-industrial growth began somewhat later than European cities as a whole. However, this may be an artifact of operationalizing "urbanization." The European urbanization trend shown in Figure 5 represents both the growth in population of cities over 20,000 and the inclusion of additional cities within this aggregate urban population when each reached 20,000.

------

[32] Higher urban mortality would have tended to draw population from rural areas to the cities simply to sustain the exsting urban-rural population ratio.

If pre-industrial European population increased as is
demonstrated in Figure 5, one must look toward examining
(1) its cause(s); (2) any factors which altered the
homeostatic level; and/or (3) the role of demographic
factors in reinstating a homeostatic equilibrium. At that
point, the rural-urban population parameters may be
examined.

The main factor now held responsible for the
population increase was the reduction in the late feudal
high mortality rate. The high death rate throughout Europe
was caused by recurring epidemics (dysentry, small pox,
typhus, but especially the plague), famine, and war
(Helliener, 1967: 72-74, 81-85). One reason proposed for
the reduced death rate was the passing of the recurring
plagues. Of course this does not explain why the
population continued to grow far beyond the peak reached in
the early fourteenth century (see Figure 5). Helliener
attributes the demise of the plague to evolutionary changes
which replaced the black rat (Mus rattus) with the brown
rat (Mus norvegicus) because the flea species Nosopsyllus
fasciatus, which is a parasite of the brown rat and unlike
the black rat's flea, "is a much less efficient vector of
the plague bacillus, and has, furthermore, little or no
appetite for human blood" (1967: 85). Even if this only a
partial explanation (or even untenable as Cipolla, 1976:

157, seems to suggest), it is likely that "some obscure ecological revolution" which caused "the deadliest among the microbes [to stop] . . . its nefarious activities" (Cipolla, 1976: 157) must have taken place.

Medical care probably did not reduce the death rate until the eighteenth century (Helliener, 1967: 89-91). Dietary improvement, inferred from differential rates of increase in disaggregated food prices, may have encouraged a greater proportion of protein in the diet even in the face of falling real wages. The argument is that grain prices rose faster than dairy, livestock, and egg prices--see Figure 6.

Before the price revolution, plague survivors may have improved their diets as a result of a relatively larger per capita supply of meat, assuming that the human mortality rate was greater than that of livestock (Helliener: 1967: 70). According to Helliener, were this the case, fertility may not have risin as many peasants may have been reluctant to "calmly face a return to porridge and rye bread, which encumbrance with a large family would entail" (Helliener, 1967: 70). While this hypothesis may not be tenable after about 1500, some change in food consumption may have been an economic factor which established a lower homeostatic population size. If this correct, it would help account for the lengthy period of population "stagnation" between

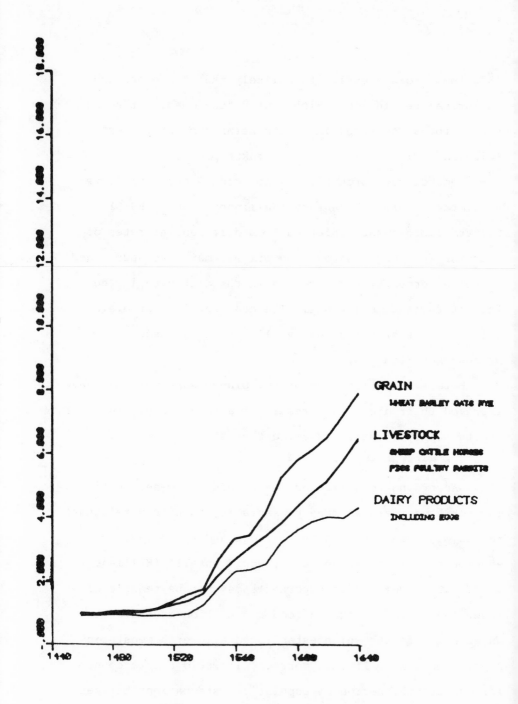

FIGURE 6:   Disaggregated Food Prices
Twenty-year Moving Average (1450-99=1.00)
Source: based on Bowden, 1967:   861-62

the Black Death and the beginning of the price revolution. Environmental and/or dietary factors which tended to decrease mortality, coupled with the hypothesized lower homeostatic population size, could have been responsible for an overshooting in the return to population homeostasis. This would also be true if the diet hypothesis is wrong and (as the homeostatic model would allow) fertility increased in response to the plague. The latter explanation better fits the demographic transition model of population growth in that it allows for a period of high mortality and high fertility to precede a period of low mortality and high fertility.

If economic change in consumption patterns is capable of lowering the homeostatic size of the European population, might not changes in production have just the opposite effect, cancelling and even reversing the trend toward a lower homeostasis? We know that in England, especially, the enclosure of open fields resulted not only in increased production of wool, but in the increased agricultural productivity of enclosed fields. While the peasants were dislocated from newly established pasture lands, is it not possible that meat and more intensively cultivated cereals entered the market to feed the growing urban population? And even if Helliener's speculation on diet choice and reproductivity is correct, those peasants who had been forced from the lands likely had no choice but to endure a marked dietary retrogression due to diminished purchasing capacity--regardless of family size.

This line of reasoning suggests that European population expansion in the urban sector was fuelled by migration, not urban fertility. We know from contemporary sources addressing social unrest that migration to the cities was a prominent feature of late feudal society. Rural economic change, especially the English enclosure movement, stimulated migration. But flight from the plague also caused considerable migration, especially in France, Italy, and Spain (Helliener, 1967: 14). Moreover, the urban death rate (both infant mortality and the crude death rate) was very high--so high that the rate of natural increase (the difference between the crude birth and death rates) in most cities was near zero.

To return to the rat hypothesis, it is clear that the plague and other epidemics assaulted areas with high population densities much more effectively due, in part, to disease communicability and poor sanitation. This means that with the passing of the period of recurrent plagues, the urban mortality rate probably dropped more appreciably than did rural mortality. However, the relatively smaller urban population would easily be multiplied several times over by even a modest rural overflow from areas unchecked by plague or famine. While it is likely that an increase in the urban rate of natural increase, due to lower mortality, and cities also grew from migration, there was not necessarily an increase in urban fertility. As is clear from Figure 5, and in keeping with the timing of the end of the series of plague epidemics, urban growth accelerated immediately after the seventeenth century crisis had passed.

In addition to disease, two other important factors acted to maintain high mortality through (and beyond) the sevententh century. Putting an end to famine and warfare would also be expected to increase the population of Europe completely independent of fertility.

Famine struck in a number of places on a number of occasions prior to and during the seventeenth century crisis period. Some of this was no doubt due to environmental factors beyond human control. Some famines were due to, or exacerbated by, inequities in the organization of production and the distribution of foodstuffs. We know, too, that famines often came in rapid succession. For example, Naples saw six famines in the last forty years of the sixteenth century. New Castile also saw six famines in a period of less than sixty years in the late sixteenth and early seventeenth centuries. These, and likely many other famine periods, were also associated with epidemic diseases (Helliener, 1967: 28).

However, while dearth has probably always served to limit

population growth, by the late sixteenth and early

seventeenth centuries in Europe, alternatives to famine

were becoming economically feasible. Some of the wealthier

and more far-sighted municipalities had begun to store

grain for such exigencies. In addition, as intra-European

trade increased far beyond its pre-mercantile limits, the

shipment of grains around the continent came to be an

alternative to starvation (Helliener, 1967: 76-78). Of

course, such grain had a price and not all the hungry could

afford it. Referring back to Figure 2, one might infer

that the fall in real wages must have had a terrible impact

upon the wage-earning classes in those periods of local

food shortage. Theft or starvation may have been the only

alternatives to paying high prices for imported foodstuffs.

According to Wrigley, "the level of real income enjoyed by

a population played a great part in determining its death

rate" (1969: 129). An adequate income not only warded off

starvation but adequate diet, clothing, and housing tended

to make for a more healthy population.

Beyond the health-threatening factors of dearth and

disease, war also had an important impact upon mortality

rates. In fact, it may be impossible to completely

separate their joint impact (Helliener, 1967: 72).

Warfare frequently led to the spread of disease and the destruction of crops; attempts to escape famine or dearth could lead to conflict and war; and where none of these existed and population grew, there is evidence from both Germany and England that warfare was publicly advocated as a means of remedying "overpopulation" (Hellenier, 1967: 30-31). While warfare certainly claimed its share of civilian victims, the gender-specific quality of European warfare also contributed to abnormal sex ratios of the warring societies. We have statistical evidence of this from Finland dating from the beginning of the eighteenth century (Helliener, 1967: 59). Through the seventeenth century and into the present, there has been little meaningful amelioration in this cause of death, the one most amenable to social intervention. "In Europe," says Cipolla (1976: 200) "war was as endemic as plague."

Conclusion

Considered in light of the homeostatic model, socio-economic and environmental antecedents of the seventeenth century crisis, contradictory though they sometimes were, are given a logical underpinning. The model allows one to articulate environmental change resulting in decreased disease with the expansion of international commerce which helped assure a minimal food

supply even in years of local crop failures. These
together tended to lower the death rate. We can now also
see how the rural economic changes precipitated by the
fourteenth century population crisis, as discussed in a
previous chapter, ultimately fuelled pre-industrial
migration and urbanization, thus freeing former serf
laborers for industrial employment under the incipient
capitalist mode of production.

CHAPTER IX

COLONIZATION, FORCED LABOR, AND TRANS-ATLANTIC
MIGRATION

The present chapter outlines colonization and the
trans-Atlantic movement of forced labor in the period which
immediately preceded the era of industrial capitalism.
Forced labor was favored as the primary means of organizing
colonial production in the Americas from approximately 1500
until well into the first half of the nineteenth century.
This period also saw the emergence of important structural
changes within the Atlantic economy with the ascendency of
slavery and indentured service over the traditional
economic practices of the Americas.

The clearing of North America by free Europeans and
indentured servants began in the early seventeenth century.
While Britain colonized North America, England came to
attain world hegemony in the aftermath of the seventeenth
century crisis and England's bourgeois revolution. In
North America in particular, the cornerstones of the
colonial economy--forced Indian labor, black slavery,
British settlement, and European indentured
servitude--were, each in its own way, antecedents of wage

labor. These cornerstones congealed into a system of free
wage labor in the nineteenth century to serve as the
foundation of modern capitalist production. In this
chapter, I address pre-capitalist settler colonization and
the movement of forced labor as important features of
migration. I also examine Africa-America slave migration
in light of England's power and needs within the emergent
world economy--particularly the need for markets and raw
materials.[33] An important issue addressed in this
chapter is the analysis of the various forms of
colonization and colonial labor organization on the basis
of a structural model of socio-economic factors suggested
by the homeostatic hypothesis.

The central feature of migration in the period
addressed by the present chapter demands a transnational
unit of analysis. International migration should not be
seen as primarily immigration or emigration with respect to
a given country, but as a transnational phenomenon. While
certain environmental factors continued to act, like
inclement weather which caused crop failure or pestilence
causing epidemic, these factors were localized--not
systemic in nature. Long-distance trade, colonization, and
mercantilist ideology and practice were not localized--they

---

[33] On the applicability of this to Africa, see Dike
(1956: 13).

were inherently transnational and essentially systemic.
Therefore, I look toward systemic socio-economic factors to
explain the general patterns of trans-Atlantic migration in
the colonial period.

Hypothesis Nine

Coerced migration was a precondition for the development of
industrial capitalism in North America.

Discussion: Slavery and Servitude: Antecedents of Wage Labor

The central hypothesis of the present chapter is that
coerced migration of laborers to the Americas--if not
slavery, per se--was one necessary condition for the
emergence of the Atlantic economy as it appeared on the eve
of the industrial capitalist epoch. The structural discord
within the European economy, especially Britain vis-a-vis
Iberia, dictated the differential patterns of forced labor
and trans-Atlantic migration which appeared in the
sixteenth through the eighteenth centuries. The loci of
slavery and indentured servitude in the Americas helped
determine the most viable sites for the development of
capitalism there.

The wage labor upon which capitalism rested emerged
first where free immigrants and indentured workers (unlike
slaves) could enter the open labor market. Capitalist

development proceeded on far less firm footing in areas where slavery persisted due to the inability of most slaves to enter into the free wage labor market. Even when slavery had been abolished, the racial-caste system required under the slave mode of production as it appeared in much of the Americas continued to operate, further smothering the potential for a free work force of wage laborers bound to neither land nor master. The possibility of wage labor developing in areas where non-class societies persisted was even slighter, still. In summary, capitalism developed first where labor had been imported and was most readily freed to enter the wage labor work force.

I shall demonstrate in the context of the structural discord within the European political economy that slavery and servitude were antecedents of wage labor in the Americas. Each form of forced labor was associated with the respective modes of production of Iberia and Britain undergoing transition to capitalism. Petty commodity production served as the mode of production which mediated feudal and capitalist production within a national unit, the most prominent example being Britain. Mercantilism served as the ideology which articulated various nations and modes of production at the transnational level in the great period of the transition to capitalism.

The slave trade and mercantilism were inseparable--to borrow a biological metaphor, they were symbiotic.[34] Without the mercantilists' orientation toward the enhancement of national wealth by the net import of bullion--as distinct from the individual merchant's profit from selling high at home what was acquired low abroad--European sponsorship of the slave trade between Africa and the Americas would have made little economic sense compared with the more profitable spice trade.[35] Without the wealth extracted from the blood and soil of Africa and the Americas, the mercantilists could probably not have accumulated the capital necessary to complete the transition from feudalism to capitalism, at least not where, when, and as it did take place--European rural accumulation notwithstanding.

The imposition of slavery--a pre-capitalist, but still class system--upon the largely primitive communal, non-class systems of the Americas established and institutionalized a propertyless and unfree work force.

---

[34] "The rise and fall of mercantilism is the rise and fall of slavery" (Williams, 1966: 136).

[35] It is important to stress the structural difference between profits made in trade which mainly altered the distribution of wealth within a given country (perhaps giving rise to internal structural change) and the direct extraction of surplus value from other countries by means of forced labor, unequal exchange, or outright plunder. The transnational dimension is what contributed to the accumulation of national wealth.

Such a work force of slaves vis-a-vis indiginous peoples facilitated the emergence of wage labor in the development of the capitalist labor process in the colonies.[36]

Iberia and the Afro-Mediterranean Economy

The economic activities of the Iberian states, particularly New Castile and Portugal, played a pivotal role in the period between the Black Death and the onset of European colonization of the Americas. Alongside capitalist development in England, Spanish and Portuguese colonization helped engender the modern phenomenon of international labor migration. In order to grasp the fundamental nature of the social and economic changes which Spain and Portugal helped to bring about, I must review several aspects of Iberian society and economy in the feudal and late feudal periods.

One significant point to be made is that the Spanish states and Portugal were perhaps as much oriented toward Africa, the Mediterranean, and Asia as they were toward Europe proper, even well into the period of American

---

[36] Similar to Walter Rodney's (1967) observation that stateless societies were not good sources of slaves because there was no ruling class to act as accomplice to the European slave traders, indigenous American non-class societies, many of which were met with European colonists, would not be expected to be good sources of either slave or wage labor. These societies lacked the class-based system of social control required by capitalism.

colonization. Like other European countries, the Iberian states participated in the spice trade with the East. Prior to the sixteenth century, Spain and Portugal were tied to the African economy through trade. Gold and slaves were traded to the enrichment of the Iberian merchants (Braudel, 1967: 402; Dike, 1956: 1) and their Italian bankers. Usher (1931) and others who argue to minimize the impact of bullion imports on the sixteenth century inflation--because inflation began before significant quantities of American treasure arrived--may have overlooked the possibility that silver from the Americas supplemented (and finally displaced) the importation of African gold. A more important element of the Afro-Mediterranean economy than gold, however, was slavery--especially when considered from a demographic perspective.

Slavery was an important feature of the Iberian and Afro-Mediterranean economies in two ways. From as early as 1444 (Donnan, 1930: 1), the slave trade was a source of profit to the Portuguese and other international merchants. The Atlantic slave trade, in about the year 1518, extended from the west coast of Africa to the Canary and other south Atlantic islands and then to Iberia and into the Mediterranean. The five-century old overland transport routes of captives destined for the slave trade terminated

along the northern and western coasts of Africa.[37]
Slavery was also important as a mode of production.
Slavery was one means used to replace serf labor lost to
plague, war, or famine--or driven out in the Reconquista.
The social relations of slavery differed significantly from
those of feudalism, particularly feudalism as it evolved in
England.

   Both the Spanish and the Portuguese engaged in the
slave trade though Portugal was more aggressive in its
pursuit. According to Rich (1967: 307-311), Portugal not
only engaged in the intercontinental trade in human beings,
but began to take the place of the Muslim traders in the
intra-African slave trade. Portuguese slave traders in
West Africa tried to monopolize this wretched business and
consequently, "the Portuguese posts caused considerable
migration among the negroes and [the] development of
migrant and de-tribalized communities, dependent on the
European posts" (Rich, 1967: 329). Bell (1974: 105)
finds that 1448-55 saw a great increase in the Portuguese
slave trade though Bell also notes that from 1441 on, there
had been many expeditions down the West African coast and

---

[37] The capture of Europeans, however, was not unknown:
as late as 1537, fifteen to eighteen thousand
inhabitants of Corfu were "abducted into slavery" by the
Turks (Helliener, 1967: 40). This must have
constituted a large part of the island's population
which was only 37,000 in 1488.

that black slaves were taken to Portugal where they were supposedly assimilated (1974: 79). Assimilation, however, must not have been the rule. Sixteenth century evidence indicates that some number of black slaves were not assimilated, in that their inadequate burial in common graves on the outskirts of Lisbon constituted a sanitation problem (Oliveira Marques, 1971: 273). The inference I draw from this is that while slaves were insignificant in numbers in Portugal from the twelfth to the fifteenth centuries, by the sixteenth, African slaves were dying in greater numbers than could be coped with by customary practices which provided for the relatively sanitary disposal of non-Christian corpses. So much for assimilation. By that time, slaves (Africans, mulattoes, Asians, and Muslims not expelled by the Reconquest) constituted some ten percent of the population of Lisbon and other parts of Portugal (Hanson, 1981: 64). Other European countries did not enter the slave trade until the mid-sixteenth century. England, for example, saw its first slave expedition to Africa in 1562 with John Hawkins (Williams, 1966: 30).

One might argue that the importance of slavery to the Afro-Mediterranean economy in this period could be overstated--slavery had probably not been a dominant mode of production in the region since classical antiquity.

Slavery in parts of Africa and southern Europe, where it existed in the late feudal period, could be said to have been a "contamination" of other modes of production. However, its existence and its legitimacy (under certain conditions) lent the expansionist Iberians knowledge and experience with a form of labor organization which seemed to maximize profitability in both the recruitment of the work force (the slave trade) and in the production of raw materials. This was of great importance as the Spanish and Portuguese established plantations and mines on the islands of the southeast Atlantic and the Caribbean and on the mainlands of the Americas.

Latin American Colonization

The general history of the colonization of the Americas is well-known. Fifteenth and sixteenth century colonization, led by Portugal and Spain, was motivated mainly by trade, not settlement (Rich, 1967: 302). What I wish to focus on here, however, are the population movements and associated modes of production of the period immediately prior to the bourgeois epoch. Of particular interest are slavery and mercantilism as means of capital accumulation and the slave trade as a population movement. One central feature of the discordant structure of the European political economy was that while Spain and

Portugal were the leading colonial powers before the seventeenth century crisis, their hegemony came into conflict with the emergent maritime economies of England and Holland. Specifically, profits from the slave trade were essential for the emergence of mercantilism and as such contributed to the economic power of the Iberian states. However, once established, mercantilism based upon slavery lacked the potential for rapid capital accumulation which was characterized by mercantilism based upon emergent capitalism, in England in particular. The strength of English mercantilism and commodity production allowed for England's incursion into, and gaining control of, the still lucrative slave trade and the subsequent incorporation of slave colonies into the British Empire. In other words, Iberian mercantilism was a variant of the Afro-Mediterranean economy of centuries past--the bastard offspring of feudalism and slavery--while English mercantilism was derived from petty commodity, nascent capitalist production. The seventeenth century crisis effectively hoisted emergent English capitalism to the dominant position within the world economy, over feudalism and all other pre-capitalist modes of production.

The Iberian powers at first sought American riches as they had those of Asia and Africa. The Spanish and Portuguese, however, came to realize that the strategies necessary to acquire and market American gold and silver differed from the pursuit of Asian spices. They concluded that trade, alone, would not yield the maximum potential profit from the Americas. The Iberians, therefore, turned to production in the Americas—the first Europeans to do so. Mining and sugar production were foremost in the economy introduced to Latin America by the Iberian colonial powers. The models of labor organization imposed upon the mines and sugar plantations of the Americas were based upon those known to the Spanish and Portuguese: Iberian-style feudalism and Canary Island-style slavery.

The indiginous American Indians were the first laborers the Spanish and Portuguese attempted to enlist (Elliott, 1963: 68-73; Hillgarth, 1972: 582). The Spanish instituted the encomendero system which was an attempt at imposing a feudalistic relation between the Indians and Spaniards. In principle, Indian property rights were to be respected though indigenous concepts of property were incompatible with European. In fact, the encomendero system disentegrated into Indian slavery. For various reasons, however, the system of forced Indian labor proved to be unviable. Not only was the mortality rate excessive, but Indians were able to effectively oppose encomendero service by desertion. In addition, forced Indian labor was opposed by the Church and by Ferdinand and

Isabella; the church of ideological and the crown for practical reasons. The Spanish king and queen were "determined to prevent the growth in the New World of those feudal tendencies which had for so long sapped the power of the Crown in Castile" (Elliott, 1963: 73). Largely for this reason, the encomendero system and Indian slavery had ended by the 1560s. Indian labor had by then been replaced with African slave labor. The reason, Mannix and Cowley (1962: 6) assert, was that African societies were more easily enslaved because of their "relatively advanced culture." This is evidently a reference to the class stratification of many African societies with which the Europeans came in contact vis-a-vis the non-class nature of many indiginous American societies.

Black slaves were used from almost the beginning--from the first decade of the sixteenth century (Hillgarth, 1978: 582; Donan, 1930: 14). The first black slaves taken to the Americas were selected from those already enslaved in Iberia. It was not until 1518 that black slaves were carried to the West Indies directly from Africa (Mannix and Cowley, 1962: viii). This systematic and massive forced displacement of population from continent to continent, an Iberian innovation rooted in the traditional Afro-Mediterranean economy, was the precursor to the development of an international division of labor and corresponding patterns of world migration.

For about the first century and a half of the colonial
period, the New World was colonized by means of
slavery--mainly by the Portuguese in Brazil and the
Spaniards in Mexico and the Caribbean, following the papal
division of the world and the subsequent Treaty of
Tordesilla. The demand for slaves in these areas, while
much less than the demand from the middle of the
seventeenth century until the early nineteenth, was
significant enough to occupy Portuguese (mainly) and other
European "merchants." While there is no way to know just
how many Africans were transported to the New World
(Donnan, 1930: 17, estimates as many as 10,000 per year by
1540), a great many were captured and sold to Spanish
colonists under the asientos system whereby the Spanish
crown sold contractural rights to non-Spaniards to supply
Spanish colonies with black slaves. This period did not
represent a qualitative change in the mode of production.
While the use of slave as opposed to serf labor in the
Americas grew, the organization of production was still
essentially pre-capitalist and rooted in the
Afro-Mediterrean economy.

Anglo-American Colonization

From the first decade of the seventeenth century,
England joined the ranks of colonial powers with its
permanent settlements in North America. English settler
colonization, however, differed from that of Spain and
Portugal, reflecting, in my view, the structural discord
within the European system: the different directions of
colonization within Europe and the different traditions of
social control in the late feudal period. Many English
colonists who began to clear the forests of North America
were planted there in communal units, free of feudalistic
seignioral ties but often bound to religious orders. This
was distinct from the Spaniards in particular who sent
soldiers responsible for exploration and the supervision of
production under forced conditions of labor.[38] Another

---

[38] Communal vis-a-vis forced labor could be said to
demonstrate the different degrees of oppression in the
period of feudal decline. The Spanish and Portuguese
orientation toward pre-capitalist forms of labor
organization seemed to follow from the intensification
of feudal oppression taken in Iberia and Eastern Europe
in the response to the feudal crisis. On the one hand,
while the British did utilize slavery which they learned
from the Spaniards, the typical settler colony
represented the severence of the feudal bond, not unlike
the loosening of feudal ties in the period of European
colonization. Taking the analogy one step further, one
might argue that the clearing of North America and the
European settlement of Indian lands was an extension of
the European colonization movement in those feudal
periods when population began to exceed its homeostasic
limit. While the pre-capitalist nature of clearing and
settlement has long since passed, the clearing of land

important difference was that the British colonizers
encouraged the migration of women which tended to
circumscribe amalgamation of colonizers and Indians. The
Spanish soldiers, however, were known to intermarry with
Indian women to further complicate the Latin American
social order.

Being relatively free of feudal forms of social
control, the first waves of petty commodity producing
British settlers, as a class, represented the transition
from feudalism to capitalism. Generally, however,
organized communities which were settled were inadequately
supplied with labor. Therefore the British introduced
another major form of forced labor during the
pre-capitalist colonial period: indentured servitude.[39]
The victims of indentured servitude were European (most
were from the British Isles) and as poor people they were
often surreptitiously "spirited away" to service in the New
World. Prisoners, as well, were transported to the
colonies for service. Given the circumstances under which
they migrated, there is no reliable way of knowing just how
many such persons made the passage. The first British use
of indentured servants coincided with the establishment of

---

and destruction of Indian society continues under
capitalist conditions of exploitation.

[39] Indentured service could be said to be a variant of
apprenticeship in some cases.

the first permanent British settlements in the New World.[40] Williams (1966: 10) cites Bacon on the advocacy of emigration in a 1606 state paper for James I. This was the period before the industrial revolution but after the enclosure movement had begun and there was fear of "overpopulation." Bacon was not the only advocate of emigration in the first decade of the seventeenth century.[41] While the conditions of servitude may have resembled those of slavery, and the high mortality rate of the indentured workers may have rivalled that of the slaves, indentured servants were to be freed once the contract was completed. The period of the contract varied according to how one entered into service: from at least seven years for convicts, to an average of two years for a redemptioner who was unable, once landed, to raise the cash to repay the complete cost of passage.

While there is some indication that Indian slavery was unsuccessfully attempted in New England as well as in the Spanish colonies, the emigration of poor whites under less-than-free conditions of labor continued well into the eighteenth century. "This emigration was in tune with

---

[40] One shipment arrived in Virginia as early as 1609 (Hansen, 1961: 28-29), just ten years before the arrival of the first black slaves in Jamestown (Greenleaf, 1970: 22).

[41] See Robert Gray, A Good Speed to Virginia reprinted in Thirsk and Cooper (1972: 757-758).

mercantilist theories of the day which strongly advocated putting the poor to industrious and useful labor and favored emigration, voluntary or involuntary, . . ." (Williams, 1966: 9-10). While such trafficking continued for a century or more, from the middle of the seventeenth century it was to be overshadowed (economically and probably demographically) by England's participation in the slave trade. Indeed, according to Williams (1966: 19), profits made in the recruitment of indentured servants were invested in the slave trade: "Capital accumulated from the one financed the other. White servitude was the historic base upon which Negro slavery was constructed." The English rise to dominance in the slave trade and the increase in the recruitment of indentured servants were rooted in the seventeenth century crisis.

The Seventeenth Century Crisis

The seventeenth century European crisis is primarily of interest here because of the changes it signalled in international migration. In order to grasp its tremendous demographic implications, however, it is necessary to review the political economy of the crisis.

Political Economy of the Crisis

The beginning of the crisis is marked by, in Hobsbawm's (1954a: 38) words, "the complex territory of price history." According to Hobsbawm, a slump set in about 1620, reaching "its most acute phase between 1640 and the 1670s" (1954a: 38). The recovery was erratic with political and environmental factors confounding recovery in different countries though towards the end of the first quarter of the eighteenth century the crisis had passed. By this time, the Iberian kingdoms had had their powers eclipsed by the Dutch and the English with England poised to take its role as the leading world power.

The so-called seventeenth century crisis was not a typical economic slump or even a depression like that of the 1930's. Instead, for a period of about one hundred years, from the first quarter of the seventeenth century, a number of European countries underwent political upheaval and structural economic change. Most notable was that of England where the bourgeoisie wrested state power from the feudalists. In the European economy, itself, the center of power shifted from Italy to England--a structural change which had been in gestation for several centuries.

This period was many-facited, complex, and contradictory. It would be impossible to fully address the crisis period here. What I wish to focus on are the main features which directly or indirectly bore upon international migration. Much of the interpretation which follows derives from Hobsbawm (1954a; 1954b).

Hobsbawm (1954a) cites four basic factors, the importance of which varied among countries, which together hindered the continued economic and population growth of the sixteenth century. These basic causes of the crisis were: (1) inadequate development of the home market in countries and areas where post-feudal (proto-industrial) production had begun to take place; (2) the use of relatively large sums of accumulated capital in finance or in the production of commodities with little market potential; (3) the expansion of agricultural production under archaic feudal conditions; and (4) failure to develop growing overseas markets for European manufactures and the falling profitability of colonial production.

The English Home Market

The English peasantry, as well as that in other European countries, continued to labor under more or less oppressive feudal conditions. However, by the use of the "putting-out system" the cottage industries were able to increase production while, having access to land, these households needed to purchase few subsistence commodities.

Rural production of textiles (for example) expanded but the rural market did not. Add to this the decline in real wages (discussed in the previous chapter) and it is likely that the wage-earning class did not provide an expanding market for its own proto-industrial manufactures.[42]

This situation contributed to a seeming overpopulation in the early seventeenth century as the existing home market for manufactured goods could be met with the employment of only a part of the population made redundant by the enclosure movement and increased agricultural productivity.

Capital Accumulation and Feudal Consumption

Not unlike the English case, the Italian market for locally produced textiles probably did not expand, either. Moreover, Hobsbawm (1954a: 42-43) refers to Italy in this period as having "feudal capitalists." The "16th century

---

[42] One reason the working class is unlikely to have provided an expanding market for its own industrial products is the long secular fall in real wages from the mid-fifteenth to the mid-seventeenth century. See Brown and Hopkins (1957) Figure 2 for Alsace, French, and Southern English building craft wages expressed as a composite physical unit of consumables. While the population size is believed to have increased in this period (thus implying a larger market), no one is certain of the rate of employment. Available evidence suggests that many of the workers were un- or underemployed, thus--especially as the buying power of wages diminished--food, rather than industrial manufactures, would likely have been first on the workers' shopping lists.

Italians probably controlled the greatest agglomerations of capital, but misinvested them flagrantly" (Hobsbawm, 1954a: 42). By this Hobsbawm meant that a large amount of the bullion which entered Iberia from Africa and America bound for Europe, channelled through the hands of Genoese and other Italian bankers, was not invested for production of commodities with mass markets, but rather in the production of luxury and artistic items. In addition, as international bankers during the price revolution, many Italian creditors who controlled a substantial portion of the bullion which entered into circulation failed to invest it in the production of anything, lending it instead, and taking long-term losses from inflation which favors debtors. Moreover, Italy underwent somewhat higher rates of inflation than northern Europe making Italian textile exports less competitive than those of England or Flanders where, in addition, the cheaper "new draperies" were made. Italian guilds refused to adopt these new techniques of textile production (Frank, 1978: 70-71). The situtation in Italy is part of the reason for the fall of Italy and the rise of England as consequences of the crisis period.

Eastern European Feudalism

I have noted the two general orientations of feudal Europe in the post-fourteenth century period. In Eastern

Europe and Iberia, where feudal oppression was intensified, feudalism was seemingly strengthened. However, in the face of an expanding European economy, international commerce was increasing, transportation and communication were improving, and significant western and northern markets for Baltic wheat developed. These markets were supplied in no small part because of the intensifiction of exploitation of the Eastern European serf. Paradoxically, this access to western markets helped to sustain the archaic mode of production as a lasting form of labor organization while at the same time concentrating economic power in fewer hands. The concentration created the preconditions for accumulation of capital in the hands of the holders of the large estates but also the preconditions for labor emigration as the feudal obligations remained severe. As the industrial revolution developed, wage labor was needed in other parts of the (by then) capitalist world.

The Colonial Markets

Colonialism and economic expansion driven by mercantilism were self-limiting. The mercantilist orientation toward a national net inflow of bullion meant that, theoretically, external sources of gold and silver would eventually become exhausted or, as was the case, become more expensive to exploit. This took place in the context of rising prices in Europe (fuelled by the massive influx of African and American specie?) such that the costs of outfitting the expeditions increased, the costs of acquiring the treasure increased, but the value of the treasure imported into Europe fell. "The benefit which Europe drew from these initial conquests was thus in the nature of a single bonus rather than a regular dividend. When it was exhausted, crisis was likely to follow. Among the colonial powers costs and overheads rose faster than profits" (Hobsbawm, 1954a: 45).

Equally, if not more important, the first period of colonization did not effectively develop markets for European manufactures. It is true, guns and other such commodities were supplied to Africa in exchange for slaves though the eventual self-limiting logic of that "trade" should be obvious. Moreover, where it was used, slavery as a mode of production did not provide the most dynamic market for imported goods.

Demographics of the Crisis and Its Imperialistic Recovery

Three types of migration figured into the causation of the seventeenth century crisis. One was the re-institution of European colonization. This followed the regrowth of the population and reproduced in the post-plague era renewed territorial expansion in Europe. Secondly, and

closely related to this but colored by larger political,
religious, and ethical issues, was the 1492 completion of
the Spanish Reconquista which drove Jews and Muslims from
the Iberian Peninsula (or into slavery). Finally, in many
ways a logical extension of these migrations, came the
colonization of the Americas including the slave trade,
forced labor of the Indians and indentured servants, and
European settlement.

England's early emergence from the crisis, compared
with the recovery of other countries, facilitated the
development of British imperialist power as dominant within
the international economy. I have already noted that
England's concentration on production rather than finance
was part of the reason for the eclipse of the Italian
economy. However, hegemony over Spain and Portugal came
about through England's capitalistic orientation toward
mercantilism. More specifically, England's shipbuilding
prowess and willingness to engage in the slave trade, from
the middle of the seventeenth century, helped to establish
a British presence within the Spanish colonial system as
Spain concentrated upon slave production rather than the
slave trade. Portugal, leading England in its pursuit,
also engaged in the slave trade but Portugal lacked the
proto-industrial foundation upon which to build trade with
Africa. England was better able to supply the guns, iron,

textiles, and sundries which were exchanged for slaves on
the West African coast.

By gaining possession of the most profitable trade
routes--finished commodities to Africa, slaves to the West
Indies, raw materials to Europe--England was in a position
to increase its colonial possessions and monopolize the
triangular trade. The infamous trade triangle not only
resulted in a net inflow of wealth to England, the goal of
the mercantilists, but also concentrated this wealth in the
British port cities which were engaged in the trade:
London, Bristol, Liverpool, Glascow, etc. Capital so
accumulated was then readily available for investment in
production in these cities and other proximate centers of
industry like Manchester or Lancaster. While
proto-industrial development in England helped enable the
British to gain control of international trade routes, the
profits from these trade routes were then, at least in
part, ploughed back into British industry. England's
monopoly over trade with British colonies consolidated the
international division of labor which articulated African
labor with American land to produce raw materials such as
brown sugar and molasses, tobacco, and cotton. These raw
materials and those produced in England, such as iron ore,
coal, and wool, were entered into the production process in
Britian. From there, marketable commodities like refined

sugar, spirits, tobacco products, guns, shackels, iron bars, tools, and textiles were entered into the world market by British shippers. By this point, Spanish-American treasure had lost its important place in the international economy.

Mercantilist imperialism served as the means by which England recovered from the crisis. Mercantilist imperialism's origins were in the trade and commerce centered in the medieval cities of Europe and the primitive accumulation of capital which came to be concentrated in the major cities of the more advanced empires, particularly the British. This primitive accumulation of merchant capital was facilitated by the plunder, enslavement, and rule over other peoples rather than by the employment of wage labor. Merchant capital, which was not yet capitalist in the strict sense of its role in the production process, but which contained elements of a bourgeois financial system, developed and persisted unevenly across the world, superimposed upon pre-capitalist economic systems.[43] Transnational means of primitive accumulation, including piracy, the slave trade, and long-distance trade in goods

---

[43] This superimposition of elements of the capitalist sphere of exchange over pre-capitalist modes of production which had not yet fully developed their internal contradictions as had, for example, Western European feudalism, is the key to the analysis of structural discord and capitalist underdevelopment.

had their demographic counterparts in the movement of
settlers, indentured workers, soldiers, and slaves.
Finally, the internal migration of former serfs to the
Western European cities was in response to the dissolution
of feudalism in the countryside and employment
opportunities in the cities. This effected the
concentration of a surplus population of urban workers
which fuelled actual capitalist production. In the
mercantile imperialist period, it was the urbanization of
serfs in Europe and the international migration of slaves,
indentured workers, and settlers alongside transnational
commerce and production which provided the labor and
capital necessary for the onset of capitalist production.

Summary

I have tried to demonstrate the role of international
migration, particularly the role of coerced migration, in
the general transformation of the Atlantic economy. The
general argument has been that coerced migration--of slaves
and indentured workers--was a pre-condition for the
development of industrial capitalism in the Americas. The
development of capitalism, and the structural
transformation of the Atlantic economy which it signalled,
established a much higher level of population homeostasis.
One means by which higher homeostasis was met was by

increased fertility. The important point to be made here,
however, is that the uneven nature of the development of
the Atlantic economy set up preconditions for massive free
international labor migration. No longer were free
migrants to be mainly settlers, but they were to become
members of the American proletariat. The relatively free
migration of workers in the nineteenth century is the topic
of the next two chapters.

CHAPTER X

FREE TRADE AND TRANS-ATLANTIC LABOR MIGRATION

Introduction

The nineteenth century saw the flourishing of free trade and, accompanying it, the predominance of the international migration of relatively free labor. Not only did forced migration finally end but for most of the nineteenth century restrictions upon emigration and immigration were minimized. In addition, this was the first century in which U.S. immigration was enumerated and for which precise yearly totals rather than estimates are available.

The purpose of this and the following chapter is to explore trans-Atlantic labor migration in light of the homeostatic model. This preliminary and exploratory study is restricted to the period c. 1828-1902. It begins in about 1828 because that is the first year for which I have data related to U.S. railway mileage added (USRMA), a variable of singular importance, as demonstrated by Thomas (1973). For some countries, suitable series did not start

until a year or two later. After 1902, several changes in
the way the dependent variables were recorded would be
expected to unduly influence the analysis so rather than
extend the series to 1913, as most such studies do, I ended
it at 1902. In the present chapter (stage one), a
preliminary examination of immigration to the United States
from the United Kingdom, The Netherlands, Belgium, Denmark,
France, Switzerland, and Spain is conducted in light of
variables intended to represent the homeostatic model. At
this point, I am looking only to identify those variables
whose cross correlations extend beyond the statistical
confidence intervals thus demonstrating the likelihood of a
non-random association between migration to the United
States and other population and economic variables at those
significantly correlated lags. No attempt will be made to
determine the magnitude of the relationships. Nor, since
this is exploratory, is there a presumption of direction of
relationships though these findings are reported.

In stage one, a preliminary analysis is conducted by
regressing the rate of emigration from specified European
countries to the U.S. on a number of variables representing
population and economic factors. In the following chapter,
stage two, those independent variables found to be
significantly correlated with migration are further
analysed to develop a series of multivariate models

designed to demonstrate the feasibility of operationalizing population and economic variables in the context of migration from seven European countries to the United States. Again, the present chapter is not concerned with analyzing the precise correlation coefficients, but rather whether relationships are statistically significant and whether the association is direct or inverse. Nor is present chapter concerned with discussing the preliminary findings in light of additional data pertaining to specific countries. Both of these more substantive aspects of the analysis are reserved for chapter eleven.

The Homeostatic Model Operationalized

Recall that the homeostatic model suggests that population size will tend to remain stable--homeostatic--in the context of fixed environmental and socio-economic factors. The thrust of my analysis is to demonstrate that migration is a reflection of a systemic attempt to maintain population homeostasis in the context of changing socio-economic and environmental factors. The purpose here is to operationalize the homeostatic model within the limits of available data by developing and testing the relationships among certain variables intended to represent demographic and socio-economic factors. The attempt to develop environmental variables from the historical data

available was unsuccessful. The variables utilized are
defined in Table 1.

There are seven dependent variables, one for each of
the seven countries of emigration in the analysis. Each
separate dependent variable is the country-specific rate of
emigration to the U.S. according to the following formula:

$$Y=(M/P)(10,000)$$

where Y is the dependent variable, the rate of migration
from a given country to the U.S.; M is the number of
immigrants to the U.S. from the given country; and P is the
population of the given country. There are two reasons for
using this measure. For one, there was a long-term
increasing trend of both population growth and migration to
the U.S. Creating a rate of migration was one way of
arithmetically detrending the migration series. More
important, the migration rate (like the birth rate or the
death rate) is more meaningful for comparative purposes,
both over time and among countries, than the actual numbers
of migrants. Moreover, the national frontiers of some
countries changed somewhat during the period covered by
this study so changes in numbers of migrants due solely to
changes in the population of the altered territories is
partially accounted for.

TABLE 1

List of Variables

Part One: Dependent Variables
(Emigration to the United States per 100,000 Population)

YBELGIUM: From Belgium
YDENMARK: From Denmark
YFRANCE: From France
YHOLLAND: From The Netherlands
YSPAIN: From Spain
YSWISS: From Switzerland
YUK: From the United Kingdom

Part Two: Independent Variables
(Pertaining to Each Country of Emigration)

U100: Total Population Residing in Urban Areas of Over
         100,000 population
C50: Total Population Residing in Cities of 50,000 to
         100,000 population
T20: Total Population Residing in Towns of 20,000 to
         50,000 population
R20: Total Population Residing in Rural Areas and Villages
         of less than 20,000 population
IMPEXP: Imports plus Exports
IMPORTS: Imports
EXPORTS: Exports
RMA: Railway Mileage Added per year
NI: National Income
STEEL: Steel Production

Part Three: Independent Variables
(Pertaining to the U.S. or the World Economy)

USPD: U.S. Population Density
USIMPEXP: U.S. Imports plus Exports
USNI: U.S. National Income
USIMPORT: U.S. Imports
USRMA: U.S. Railway Mileage Added per year
USSTEEL: U.S. Steel Production
USPRWTRD: U.S. Proportion of World Trade
WRLDTRAD: World Trade

The independent variables are discussed below according to two basic categories: (1) demographic variables from the countries of emigration and population density of the United States; and (2) variables concerning the economies of the countries of emigration and the United States economy, and one representing the world economy. Since previous researchers (e.g. Jerome, 1926; Thomas, 1973) have demonstrated that changes in migration to the U.S. often lagged changes in the independent variables, in the preliminary stage, the dependent variables in this data set were regressed on the independent variables five times with lags of zero through four years. That is, the dependent (e.g. YSPAIN) was first regresed on each independent for the corresponding year. Next, the dependent was regresed on each independent such that the dependent variable lagged the independent by one year. The same process was repeated through four lags. This was carried out for each of the seven dependent variables. All such lagged variables which did not prove statistically significant with a t-ratio of at least 2.0 were removed from further analysis.

Hypothesis Ten

The conditions of industrial economies constitute important influences on international migration.

Among industrialized (or industrializing) countries, the state of the national economy of the country of emigration would exercise an important influence upon the patterns of migration to the U.S. However, the complexity and diversity of relationships between migration and economy, both among different countries and over time, prevents an a priori determination of the direction of the relationship.

Hypothesis Eleven

Changes in rural population size are directly related to changes in emigration.

In the late feudal, early industrial countries of Europe, migration to the U.S. would be directly influenced at least in part by changes in the size of the rural population (reflecting changes in Marx's "latent reserve army.") Migration was also subject to environmental interventions, especially inclement weather, which tended to impact migration series with sudden shocks.

Hypothesis Twelve

<u>During the transition from industrial capitalism to
imperialism, economic factors demonstrate greater influence
on international migration than do non-economic factors.</u>

Economic variables, both push and pull, would be
expected to become dominant within a multivariate model
over non-economic variables.

Hypothesis twelve derives from a variant of Marxian
theory, often associated with Lenin, which suggests that
the 1870s saw a major turning point in capitalist
development. In the early "industrial" stage, capital
accumulation was derived mainly from the export of
commodities by the most advanced capitalist countries. In
the later "imperialist" stage, capital accumulation was
derived from the export of capital for investment abroad.
If this is correct, we should be able to discern a
corresponding pattern of international labor migration.

Since England is generally understood to have been the
primary imperialist country at the conjuncture in question,
I would expect that economic variables for other countries
could assume greater importance in the imperialist stage
than in the industrial stage of capitalism. This should be
true whether we speak of net labor importing countries such
as the United States (in which case an "economic pull"

would be evident) or in net labor exporting countries. For the latter, at minimum, a diminishing of any evidence of "population push" would be expected. In addition, there should be seen a shift to economic pull factors where they were not previously evident.

Preliminary Analysis of Population Variables, Stage One

Ravenstein (1885; 1889) demonstrated that as of the 1880s, certain patterns of European internal migration had emerged. Among the more pertinent of his observations were that rural natives were more migratory than town natives. This is in keeping with the analysis of the previous chapters which addressed the factors which seem to have influenced migration in the period of the decline of feudalism. Another point Ravenstein made was that long-distance migration tended to take place in stages; that migrants would travel from their places of origin to successively larger intermediate places before reaching their final destinations. Most migration seemed to be related to job-seeking and long-distance migrants tended to move to the major cities. International migration seemed to follow the same pattern. These empirical observations in no way contradict the theoretical explanation derived from the relative surplus population thesis.

The Marxian explanation suggests that one important sector of the relative surplus population--the latent reserve army--inherently represents a migrant population: displaced peasants forced to migrate to the towns and cities. A second component of the relative surplus population--the floating reserve--could be said to be potentially migratory as workers made redundant in one industry have often found it necessary to migrate to another place to find work in the same or a new industry. Finally, the "stagnant reserve" could be viewed as those displaced peasants and their descendants who had settled in urban areas but remained unemployed.

Under this general scheme, the latent reserve should be found migrating from rural areas to nearby towns and in some cases bound for an overseas destination. The floating reserve, as migrants, would be found moving from smaller towns to larger and from the largest urban areas to overseas destinations. The stagnant reserve would not be expected to migrate. According to the homeostatic hypothesis, the ultimate causes of such migration would be environmental or social structural. The immediate cause may appear to be demographic, e.g. population pressure, but there should be environmental and/or socio-economic roots to the immediate demographic cause of migration. I believe that the primary environmental cause of migration was adverse weather which affected crops, setting in motion latent reserve elements of the peasantry. This hypothesis cannot be properly operationalized and tested though Brinley Thomas's (1973: 168) examination of Swedish emigration data seems to demonstrate a correspondence between emigration and poor harvests. The potato blight and the resultant Irish famine, though by no means a solely enviromental phenomenon, represents another example of environmental factors at work. Still another hypothesized cause of migration would be the ebb and flow of economic activity. This is one social structural element I shall examine in the next section.

Following Ravenstein (1885; 1889), whose analysis allowed him to draw general conclusions about internal migration on the basis of census and other data, I would expect migration to a take place from smaller places to larger places and from both rural and urban areas to overseas destinations. This pattern suggests that as population grows--because of higher fertility, lower mortality, or net in-migration--where urban places are least able to absorb greater numbers (e.g. through an alteration of homeostasis by means of changing economic factors) there would be a tendency toward emigration.

With regard to demographic components of population growth, I have only indirect evidence. I cannot

independently measure the effects of differential rates of
fertility or mortality nor can I measure the net migration
into or out of specific cities.   I can, however, measure
the net impact of these three demographic factors on
population size. The population of each country of
emigration is divided into the following gradations: the
population residing in urban areas of over 100,000 (U100);
the population residing in cities of 50,000 to 100,000
(C50); the population residing in towns of 20,000 to 50,000
(T20); and the population residing in rural areas and
villages of less than 20,000 (R20).   In a few cases, for
reasons which will be explained, the size criteria differ
slightly.

Preliminary Findings

The preliminary results of the dependent population
variables regressed on the independent population and
economic variables in stage one of this analysis are to be
found in Table 2. Not all variables had values for the
entire period from the late 1820s to 1902. For this
reason, and because a structural change in the world
economy seems to have taken place in about the 1870s, the
entire period is divided into pre-1878 and post-1876, early
and late periods. The dividing point, 1877, is in some
respects arbitrary but it derives from Thomas's (1973)

findings and an examination of British migration to the
United States. The year, 1877, marked a major trough in
British migration to the U.S. Similar major turning points
are found in other U.S. immigration series in the same or a
neighboring year.

While the urban population of the more industrial
countries of emigration has consistently increased,
indicating a continued ability to absorb surplus
population, I would expect to find no significant
correlation between emigration and U100. This may be
inferred from hypothesis ten in that the largest cities are
understood to have been the sites of the greatest
productive activity and as the loci of the greatest
employment opportunities. Any correlation between
emigration and U100 would indicate an inability of the
large cities to absorb population increases (due
substantially to migration from smaller places) and/or the
inability of the large cities to employ a large part of the
urban population.

The positive correlation, in particular, may represent
the emigration of the latent reserve populations. This is
because a positive correlation demonstrates a simple direct
relation between emigration and urbanization. Since the
bulk of the population growth in the urban areas derived
from in-migration rather urban high fertility/low

TABLE 2

Population Variables: Stage One

Dependent Variables	Independent Variables	c.1828–1902					c.1828–1877					1877–1902				
lags:		0	1	2	3	4	0	1	2	3	4	0	1	2	3	4
YBELGIUM	U100															
YDENMARK	U100			+				−	+			−				
YFRANCE	U100															
YHOLLAND	U100						+	−								
YSPAIN	U100	−														−
YSWISS	U100															
YUK	U100												+			
lags:		0	1	2	3	4	0	1	2	3	4	0	1	2	3	4
YBELGIUM	C50															
YDENMARK	C50															
YFRANCE	C50											−				
YHOLLAND	C50				−		−	+								−
YSPAIN	C50	−													−	+
YSWISS	C50	+														
YUK	C50															
lags:		0	1	2	3	4	0	1	2	3	4	0	1	2	3	4
YBELGIUM	T20												+	+		−
YDENMARK	T20			+					+							+
YFRANCE	T20											−				
YHOLLAND	T20										+		−	−		
YSPAIN	T20	+										+				
YSWISS	T20															
YUK	T20												+		−	−
lags:		0	1	2	3	4	0	1	2	3	4	0	1	2	3	4
YBELGIUM	R20															+
YDENMARK	R20				+											
YFRANCE	R20															
YHOLLAND	R20	+					+									
YSPAIN	R20															
YSWISS	R20															
YUK	R20					+	−					−	−		+	+

Table 2--<u>Continued</u>

Dependent Variables	Independent Variables	c.1828-1902					c.1828-1877					1877-1902				
		0	1	2	3	4	0	1	2	3	4	0	1	2	3	4
YBELGIUM	USPD			−	+				−	+						
YDENMARK	USPD	+														
YFRANCE	USPD	+														
YHOLLAND	USPD	+														
YSPAIN	USPD															
YSWISS	USPD															
YUK	USPD			−	+									+		

Note: "+" indicates a positive relationship at a probability less than 0.05.
"−" indicates a negative relationship at a probability less than 0.05.

mortality, with no other independent variable considered (until stage two), the positive correlation suggests the presence of an antecedent factor which motivates migration (both urbanization and emigration, alike). This could be population pressure and/or socio-economic change in the smaller places or rural areas. Therefore the positive correlation would most likely be found in less advanced countries.

A negative correlation between U100 and emigration suggests several interpretations. One would be that emigration serves as a more viable alternative to migration to the largest cities but would also indicate the presence of an additional exogenous factor (e.g. the economy) operating periodically to limit and then expand urban employment opportunities. Thus when urban economic life is improving, the propensity to migrate declines. This suggests an intervening variable between that which "causes" migration and U100, a factor which operates to channel migration into either emigration or to the largest cities. Thomas (1973) demonstrates this possibility in a study of migration from Britain to the U.S. and of the opposing economic cycles operating between the two cuntries in the period from the 1870s to World War I.

Correlation between U100 and migration strongly suggests the need for a multivariate analysis which I have conducted in the second stage. The negative correlation suggests the presence of an intervening variable; the positive, emigration of the latent reserve (from rural areas) or the floating reserve (from smaller cities).

In a number of cases, involving U100 and other variables, the preliminary analysis yielded contradictory findings between lags of the same variable with one lag being positively correlated and another being negatively correlated with migration. These anomolies are intepreted here as being due to the nature of trending in the varaibles, as artifacts of the size of the sample, or to empirical characteristics of some of the independent variables. In most cases the anomolies were resolved in a later stage of the analysis where they are discussed.

The preliminary findings largely conform to the expected results. Of the seven countries of emigration, only Denmark and Spain demonstrated a significant correlation between U100 and migration to the U.S. for the entire period. Once the second stage consisting of economic and demographic variables was brought to bear, however, U100 was no longer significant for any country for the entire period, c. 1828-1902. When the entire period was divided into an early period (pre-1877) and a late period (post-1877), the early period was found to have for Denmark and The Netherlands a U100 which was statistically significant when correlated with emigration. This suggests episode(s) of urban economic stagnation in these countries relative to the forces which encouraged emigration such that for the floating reserve, the U.S. served as a destination alternative to Amsterdam, Rotterdam, or Copenhagen; the only Dutch or Danish cities which had reached 100,000 by the middle of the century. In the post-1877 period, U100 for the United Kingdom, Denmark, and Spain was statistically significant. The U.K. finding is in keeping with those by Thomas (1973) as cited above.

There was no Swiss city over 100,000 in the ninteenth century so C50 was interpreted as being functionally equivalent to U100. C50 proved to be significant (except in the early period alone) in stage one but not in stage two.

The analysis of C50 and T20 proceeded similarly to that of U100. A positive correlation between C50 or T20 and emigration would suggest an inability of places of respectively 50,000 to 100,000 or 20,000 to 50,000 to absorb population growth fuelled by in-migration from smaller places. A negative correlation again seems to suggest the presence of economic factors operating cyclicly, generating jobs and so discouraging emigration in one phase, diminishing jobs and thus encouraging emigration in the other phase. C50 and T20 than U100. I would expect the largest places to be the most dynamic, and thus be better able to absorb population change than smaller places. That being the assumption, I would expect to find a greater number of countries demonstrating significant correlations between changes in migration and C50 or T20 than between migration and U100.

With the exception of T20 in the late period (1877-1902), the findings do not indicate any remarkable difference in the number of countries with significant t-ratios for T20 and C50. What they seem to suggest is that in the post-1877 period, economic forces operated to fetter the growth of towns of 20,000 to 50,000 population.

Spain maintains significant t-ratios for the entire period
for both gradations of population. This seems to suggest a
relative stagnation within the Spanish urban-industrial
sector. Similarly, Denmark maintains a statisticallly
significant correlation between T20 and emigration--there
being no cities with population less than Copenhagen's
135,000 and greater than 20,000 (as of mid-century). The
country which best met the expectations was The
Netherlands. For The Netherlands, C50 was statistically
significant for the entire period while T20 was significant
for the early period and the late period, but not for the
entire period fitted to one model. What this suggests is a
curvilinear relationship between emigration and T20 with
some structural change taking place, probably in the 1870s.
France demonstrated a significant correlation between both
C50 and T20 vis-a-vis emigration in the post-1877 period
alone. This suggests that the intermediate-sized French
cities and towns had begun to reach their capacities to
absorb additional population toward the end of the
nineteenth century. For T20, Belgium and the United
Kingdom also demonstrated significant t-ratios in the later
period, contributing to a general suggestion that as the
nineteenth century progressed, smaller cities and towns
were the first to reach homeostasis (given existing
economic factors) while the larger urban areas proved more

dynamic in their abilties to develop economically and grow, thus not being associated with emigration.

For France, there were sufficient data available to further sub-divide the population gradations into the following: U25 (population residing in towns of 25,000 to 50,000); U20 (population residing in towns of 20,000 to 25,000); T10 (population residing in towns of 10,000 to 20,000); and R10 (population residing in rural areas of less than 10,000). The only additional information which could be derived from the stage one analysis on the basis of these variables was that for the entire period T10 was statistically significant while R10 was not (from Table 2 it will be seen that R20 is significant), suggesting that the larger villages (over 10,000) were unable to absorb population growth while the rural areas were. This finding suggests that R20 would not be a particularly good indicator of the relationship between rural population growth and emigration due to the appearant economic heterogeneity among places within the gradation 20,000 and less. The empirical results are inconclusive. If R20 were to be an adequate measure of rural population growth, and rural population pressure were to be seen as the primary factor responsible for population movement, a distinct pattern of positive correlations would be expected. For these reasons, I must consider R20 inadequate for the intended purposes.

United States population density (USPD) was intended to indirectly measure the impact of westward expansion into Indian territories as an inducement to European farmers to emigrate. With the exception of Belgium, none of the significant variables in stage one were carried through stage two. The case of Belgium, which I discuss in detail in the next chapter, represents the intervention of randon shocks consisting of political and environmental factors in Europe which occurred coincidentially with important changes in USPD. USPD, therefore, is not seen as a meaningful independent variable.

Preliminary Analysis of Economic Variables, Stage One

Another hypothesized cause of migration would be economic activity. This is perhaps the single most studied phenomenon associated with nineteenth century trans-Atlantic labor migration. The present study differs from others in that (where data are available) it develops a number of comparable economic variables for seven countries of emigration, a number of economic variables for the U.S. as the country of immigration, and a variable intended to represent the world economy. These are in addition to the demographic variables discussed above.

This part of stage one represents an attempt to develop five categories of economic measures related to international migration. The categories are:

1. Push factors not directly related to the world economy
    (RMA, STEEL, and NI);

2. Push factors clearly related to the world economy
    (IMPEXP, IMPORTS, EXPORTS);

3. Pull factors not directly related to the world economy
    (USRMA, USSTEEL, USNI);

4. Pull factors clearly related to the world economy
    (USIMPORT, USIMPEXP, USPRWTRD);

5. A general indicator of the world economy (WRLDTRAD).

Push Factors not Directly Related to the World Economy

Brinley Thomas analysed variables similar to those
which I see as push factors related mainly to the national
economies of the countries of emigration. Thomas (1973:
Chapter XI) demonstrated that building cycles in the U.S.
and U.K. were inversely related and that major transfers of
population and capital from the U.K. to the U.S. played
important roles in determining the placement of the periods
of both economic expansion and relative stagnation
in both countries. Unfortunately, analogous data for other
countries are unavailable. Thomas also demonstrated that
cycles of British national income operated counter to
emigration. In addition, Thomas found that Swedish railway
construction was inversely related to cycles of Swedish
emigration (Thomas, 1973: 128). These measures are both

TABLE 3

Economic Variables: Stage One

Dependent Variables	Independent Variables	c.1828–1902					c.1828–1877					1877–1902				
		lags: 0	1	2	3	4	0	1	2	3	4	0	1	2	3	4
YBELGIUM	IMPEXP															
YDENMARK	IMPEXP															
YFRANCE	IMPEXP						+		+							
YHOLLAND	IMPEXP															
YSPAIN	IMPEXP	+														
YSWISS	IMPEXP															
YUK	IMPEXP	+					+									

Dependent Variables	Independent Variables	c.1828–1902					c.1828–1877					1877–1902				
		0	1	2	3	4	0	1	2	3	4	0	1	2	3	4
YBELGIUM	IMPORTS															
YDENMARK	IMPORTS															
YFRANCE	IMPORTS			+						+	+					
YHOLLAND	IMPORTS															
YSPAIN	IMPORTS	+														−
YSWISS	IMPORTS															
YUK	IMPORTS	+	−				+									

Dependent Variables	Independent Variables	c.1828–1902					c.1828–1877					1877–1902				
		0	1	2	3	4	0	1	2	3	4	0	1	2	3	4
YBELGIUM	EXPORTS															
YDENMARK	EXPORTS															
YFRANCE	EXPORTS															
YHOLLAND	EXPORTS															
YSPAIN	EXPORTS															
YSWISS	EXPORTS															
YUK	EXPORTS	+														

Dependent Variables	Independent Variables	c.1828–1902					c.1828–1877					1877–1902				
		0	1	2	3	4	0	1	2	3	4	0	1	2	3	4
YBELGIUM	RMA															
YDENMARK	RMA				+		+		−	+		−	−			
YFRANCE	RMA												+	+		
YHOLLAND	RMA								+							
YSPAIN	RMA															
YSWISS	RMA															
YUK	RMA		+	+	+	+		+	+		+		+	+		

Table 3--<u>Continued</u>

Dependent Variables	Independent Variables	c.1828-1902					c.1828-1877					1877-1902				
		0	1	2	3	4	0	1	2	3	4	0	1	2	3	4
YBELGIUM	NI															
YDENMARK	NI															
YFRANCE	NI															
YHOLLAND	NI															
YSPAIN	NI															
YSWISS	NI															
YUK	NI											+				
		0	1	2	3	4	0	1	2	3	4	0	1	2	3	4
YBELGIUM	STEEL													+		−
YDENMARK	STEEL															
YFRANCE	STEEL															
YHOLLAND	STEEL															
YSPAIN	STEEL															
YSWISS	STEEL															
YUK	STEEL															
		0	1	2	3	4	0	1	2	3	4	0	1	2	3	4
YBELGIUM	USIMPEXP												+			
YDENMARK	USIMPEXP		+		−		−									−
YFRANCE	USIMPEXP						+									
YHOLLAND	USIMPEXP	−	+		+	−	+	+		−						
YSPAIN	USIMPEXP															
YSWISS	USIMPEXP	+			−											−
YUK	USIMPEXP	+					+									
		0	1	2	3	4	0	1	2	3	4	0	1	2	3	4
YBELGIUM	USNI					+									−	+
YDENMARK	USNI						+									
YFRANCE	USNI															
YHOLLAND	USNI					+				+						
YSPAIN	USNI						+					+				
YUK	USNI											+				

Table 3--<u>Continued</u>

Dependent Variables	Independent Variables	c.1828-1902					c.1828-1877					1877-1902				
		0	1	2	3	4	0	1	2	3	4	0	1	2	3	4
YBELGIUM	USIMPORT		+										+			
YDENMARK	USIMPORT	+	+		-				+		-	+				-
YFRANCE	USIMPORT															
YHOLLAND	USIMPORT	+	+	-	-	-	+	+				+			-	-
YSPAIN	USIMPORT															
YSWISS	USIMPORT	+	+		-		+					+			-	
YUK	USIMPORT	+					+									

Dependent Variables	Independent Variables	c.1828-1902					c.1828-1877					1877-1902				
		0	1	2	3	4	0	1	2	3	4	0	1	2	3	4
YBELGIUM	USRMA	+					+									
YDENMARK	USRMA	+	+	+		+						+		+		+
YFRANCE	USRMA											+	+			+
YHOLLAND	USRMA	+		+								+		+		
YSPAIN	USRMA									-	+				-	+
YSWISS	USRMA	+	+						+			+	+	+		
YUK	USRMA											+				

Dependent Variables	Independent Variables	c.1828-1902					c.1828-1877					1877-1902				
		0	1	2	3	4	0	1	2	3	4	0	1	2	3	4
YBELGIUM	USSTEEL															
YDENMARK	USSTEEL															
YFRANCE	USSTEEL															
YHOLLAND	USSTEEL															
YSPAIN	USSTEEL															
YSWISS	USSTEEL															
YUK	USSTEEL		-													

Dependent Variables	Independent Variables	c.1828-1902					c.1828-1877					1877-1902				
		0	1	2	3	4	0	1	2	3	4	0	1	2	3	4
YBELGIUM	USPRWTRD	+		-								+				
YDENMARK	USPRWTRD															
YFRANCE	USPRWTRD			-												
YHOLLAND	USPRWTRD		+	-												
YSPAIN	USPRWTRD															
YSWISS	USPRWTRD															-
YUK	USPRWTRD															

Table 3--<u>Continued</u>

Dependent Variables	Independent Variables	c.1828-1902					c.1828-1877					1877-1902				
		0	1	2	3	4	0	1	2	3	4	0	1	2	3	4
YBELGIUM	WRLDTRAD															
YDENMARK	WRLDTRAD															
YFRANCE	WRLDTRAD	-										-				
YHOLLAND	WRLDTRAD															
YSPAIN	WRLDTRAD															
YSWISS	WRLDTRAD															
YUK	WRLDTRAD															

Note: "+" indicates a positive relationship
at a probabilty less than 0.05.
"-" indicates a negative relationship
at a probablilty less than 0.05.

available for several of the countries in the present

analysis which are reported in Table 3.

The theoretical importance of national income (NI) is

that it should be a good general measure of the state of

the economy. A positive correlation between NI and

emigration would suggest that a favorable economy provides

sufficient income to allow those already inclined to

emigrate to do so. A negative correlation suggests that

emigrants move to escape adverse economic conditions. I

would analyse railway mileage added (RMA) and steel

production (STEEL) similarly though would expect these to

be particularly good indicators of floating reserve

emigration as steel production and railway construction are both associated with a robust industrial economy and are important sources of employment. The importance of railway construction cannot be overlooked (Hobsbawm, 1977: 209-210).

As demonstrated in Table 3, no systematic correlations were found between migration and either STEEL or NI. RMA, however, was shown to be correlated at a statistically significant level with emigration from the U.K. (the early period in particular), but also with emigration from Denmark, France, and the Netherlands. The Netherlands and the U.K. both maintained statistical significance for RMA through the second stage of the analysis. These correlations were positive, as were most of the others. This suggests that RMA may be seen more as an enabling factor than a causal factor in effecting emigration.

Pull Factors Related to the World Economy

Thomas (1973: 96-99; 240-241) stressed the role of British foreign investment in developing the infrastructure of countries of immigation (especially the U.S.) and if his data are reliable, which I question, British investment overseas might best be seen as a "pull" factor.[44]

---

[44] Thomas's measure of British foreign investment is based upon Imlah (1958: 70-75). I have some serious reservations about the use of Imlah's data for time

While Thomas has demonstrated a questionable relationship between "capital exports" and emigration, he has also demonstrated the importance of all exports (Thomas, 1973: 100-102). Imports of food from the U.S. was also shown to be associated with emigration from the U.K. to the U.S. (Thomas, 1973: 180ff.) as well as to the building cycle. Of the three variables used in the present analysis, I see IMPEXP (imports plus exports) as a general indicator of the state of the economy of the country of emigration within an international setting. I see EXPORTS as a good indicator of the productive sector (industrial or agricultural, depending upon the country) and also of the availablilty of passenger transportation (from all but

---

series analysis. Thomas utilizes Imlah's "balance on current account" as the measure of foreign investment, a measure which is consistently positive from 1816 (the first year for which Imlah provides figures) through 1913, Imlah's final year. The problem arises in Imlah's construction of the current account series. The balance on current account is a summation of the net balance on trade and services with the balance on interest and dividends derived from foreign investments. It is with the balance on interest and dividends that I have problems.

The balance on interest and dividends is calculated yearly on the basis of an average estimated return on the accumulating balance of British credit abroad. Not only does Imlah assume that capital gains equalled capital losses, but he assumes a fairly constant rate of return. Equally serious, however, is the actual calculation of the accumulating credit abroad. Szymanski (1981: 104) evidently utilized Imlah's accumulating credit abroad as his measure of British capital export. The first problem facing this series is that the initial datum (for 1815): "circa 10.0?" is by

Switzerland) to overseas destinations. I see IMPORTS as a
general indicator of a robust demand for industrial and
consumer products as would be expected in a thriving
industrial or industrializing economy and thus one measure
of potential opportunities for industrial employment.

According to the results reported in Table 3, IMPORTS
proved more often to be significantly correlated with
emigration--for France, Spain, and the U.K. This was the
only variable of the three which maintained significance in
the second stage, though only for France. The French
pattern of negative and positive correlations suggests that
emigration lags IMPORTS (industrial employment) positively
by four years such that an increase in IMPORTS tends to

Imlah's admission a guess. The next problem concerns
the relative sources of accumulation before and after
1825. For the decade 1815-1825, the primary component
of accumulating credit abroad is the net balance on
trade and services which is consistently positive until
1825, with the total net balance for the decade
1816-1825 a positive 11.58 million pounds. From that
point onward through 1913, the net balance on trade and
services is a negative 156.69 million pounds. One key
issue is that by the second quinquinium of the 1820s,
the balance on interest and dividends acquired abroad
had surpassed the net balance on trade and services in
relative importance as a component of the balance on
current account. This means that from 1825, no longer
was credit abroad accumulated mainly by a surplus in
British trade and service accounts, but by interest and
dividends on credit already existing abroad. The
balance on current account, positive for every year
largely because of a consistently positive balance on
interest and dividends, was each year added to the
accumulating balance of credit abroad. What the
accumulating balance of credit abroad effectively

encourage an increase in emigration four years later with a decrease in IMPORTS similarly discouraging emigration four years later by providing or restricting savings available to finance the movement. However, IMPORTS at lag 3 is inversely related to emigration suggesting that three years prior to the actual year of migration, may have no impact upon emigrants whose decisions were made in the previous year (lag 4). Among the undecided, however, a downturn in IMPORTS would seem to encourage emigration three years hence.

---

represents, therefore, is the compound interest on British credits estimated to have been "earned" prior to 1825, diminished in the long run by the deficit in the net balance on trade and services after 1825.

For a time series analysis, what the balance on current account reflects, therefore, is Imlah's estimate of small changes in the trend of interest and dividends on credits abroad plus large changes in the balance on trade and services. The balance on current account series, Thomas's variable, does not measure foreign investment. The accumulating credit abroad, Szymanski's measure, is only a rough approximation, though probably the best available. What it measures, for the most part, is the compound interest on estimates of pre-1825 earnings from business services on foreign trade (as the balance on visible trade was negative for this first decade) minus a long term net deficit in the balance on trade and services. According to Imlah's method of estimating British balance of payments, Britain's great international economic power on the eve of its destruction in the First World War, was a result solely of primitive accumulation in the period of precapitalist

Pull Factors Not Directly Related to the World Economy

Another set of independent variables pertains to the
United States economy. Unlike the previous six
independents which had different values for each country of
emigration, the following six all used the same data from
the U.S.

The first three independent variables I shall discuss
are seen as not being directly related to the world
economy: USNI, USSTEEL, USRMA. The findings are reported
in Table 3. U.S. national income is supposed to represent
the general state of the United States economy. While we
do not know how accurately and effectively the general
state of the American economy was reported in Europe, we do
know that remittances from earlier migrants to relatives in
the "old country" played an important role in financing
further emigration. USNI, therefore, is seen as an
indicator of the ability of current immigrants to the U.S.
to finance further immigration. USSTEEL and USRMA are seen
as similar measures of the U.S. economy but especially as
indicators of the state of the industrial sector and
employment opportunities. USRMA in particular played a
major part in the Thomas (1973) analysis. I would expect

---

mercantile imperialism with interest compounded yearly.
According to Imlah's estimate, there was no net export
of capital from Britain between 1825 and 1913, thus
calling into question Imlah's data or Lenin's thesis.

all correlations to be positive though, due to the time and distance factors, some lags between the U.S. independent variables and migration would not be unanticipated.

The results were somewhat surprising. USSTEEL and USRMA were seen theoretically as rather similar variables though reference to Table 3 demonstrates that USSTEEL proved almost totally ineffective while, of all independent variables, USRMA proved to be most highly correlated with emigration. Nearly all USRMA correlations were positive, all countries had at least one lag-period specific USRMA which maintained its statistical significance through the second stage of analysis. USNI was only modestly succesful--only one country (Denmark) had a lag-period which maintained statistical significance through stage two of the analysis, and that was negative. What these findings seem to suggest is that at least some of the factors which may be inferred from USRMA (e.g. general state of the industrial sector or westward expansion), are not particularly important as other equally or more direct measures of them (e.g. USSTEEL, USPD) do not demonstrate any remarkable pattern of correlations.

Pull Factors Related to the World Economy

The next set of indepenent variables--USIMPORT, USPRWTRD, and USIMPEXP--is more directly related to the world economy. USIMPORT is seen to represent imports of capital goods (as the U.S. was a predomiantly agricultural and food exporting country) and the means of passage of immigrants as passengers aboard ships carrying cargo imports to the U.S. USPRWTRD, U.S. proportion of world trade, is seen as a general indicator of the state of the U.S. economy vis-a-vis the world economy. I would expect a positive correlation between migration and USPRWTRD as the latter represents the relative health of the American economy within the world system. USIMPEXP is seen as an indicator of the American economy, not relative to other countries but rather within the context of the world economy.

The findings demonstrate that USIMPORT is a somewhat better indicator than USIMPEXP while both are much better than USPRWTRD. This suggests that the health of the entire world economy is more important than the state of health of the U.S. within the world economy. Though four countries demonstrated some correlation between emigration and USPRWTRD, not one of these held through the second stage. Six countries demonstrated one or more lag-periods of

statistical significance for USIMPEXP and only five for
USIMPORT. However, three countries (Denmark, The
Netherlands, and Switzerland) maintained statistical
significance for USIMPORT through the second stage while
only two (Denmark and Switzerland) did so for USIMPEXP.
Both USIMPORT and USIMPEXP show an unexpected pattern of
positive and negative correlations. Both are predominantly
negative for the higher lags (three and four) than for the
lower. One possibility is that the longer lags reflect the
"stayers" who prosper from the gains derived from USIMPORT
and USIMPEXP. The shorter lags reflect more immediate
responses of migrants leaving to take advantage of
opportunities abroad. Another possible interpretation is
that even in relatively prosperous years for immigrants to
America, remittances were witheld until sufficient funds
were available to bring an entire family over.

The USIMPORT and USIMPEXP results are curiously
incongruous with the findings of USRMA, the only
independent variable which seems to have been more
important than USIMPORT. Could it be that young, single
male immigrants (or those with only a wife and no children
in their home country) tended to be employed in railway
construction and similar jobs and sent for individual
family members at the earliest possible time while the
older, middle-class, male immigrant deriving income

primarily from commerce, etc. waited until he had saved
sufficient money that his entire family could join him?
This conjecture is, of course, difficult to reconcile with
the mover-stayer approach and indicates that further
analysis is required.

World Trade as an Independent Variable

Finally, WRLDTRAD, a single independent variable
developed to represent the general health of the world
economy, is reported in Table 3. Unlike one of its
component measures (USIMPORT), but like others (IMPORTS,
EXPORTS), the indicator of world trade did not prove very
effective--only a single country (France) demonstrated a
statistically significant relationship between migration to
the U.S. and world trade (a negative one at that) though
it was not maintained through the second stage of the
analysis.

Retrospective in Hypotheses Ten through Twelve

Regarding hypothesis ten, the preliminary findings
demonstrate wide diversity in associations between the
various measures of economy and migration. In general,
U.S. economic variables (especially USRMA and USIMPORT)
demonstrate widespread correlations with the dependent
variables--USRMA with migration from each country.

Economic push varaibles demonstrated much fewer striking patterns, except for RMA. My preliminary findings tend to underscore the importance of the railway construction variables (RMA and USRMA). These findings also demonstrate the complexity and diversity of the relationships and support the need for a multivariate analysis as is reported in the following chapter.

Hypothesis eleven is not well supported by the preliminary analysis. Only four countries demonstrated significant relationships between R20 and migration: Belgium, Denmark, the Netherlands, and the United Kingdom. For all these (except the U.K.), the correlation is positive as would be inferred from the hypothesis. The probable reason for the negative association lies in the tendency of R20 to include non-rural population. Unfortunately, no more suitable measure is available.

Hypothesis twelve could not be directly addressed in the preliminary stage of the analysis because it requires a multivariate analysis, one which allows for the inclusion of both economic and non-economic variables in each model. The discussion of the differential findings for each of the periods is best held following the completion of stage two.

Conclusion

Curiously, when I compared the findings from the
analyses of USIMPORT and USPRWTRD I inferred a greater
importance for the world economy than the relative state of
the American economy. The world trade finding seems to
contradict that inference. When comparing findings from
economic push factors (IMPORTS and EXPORTS) vis-a-vis the
economic pull factor (USIMPORT), one is led to infer that
the state of the U.S. economy is more important than that
of the countries of emigration. The USRMA findings support
this.

This study is not alone in suggesting a more major
role for the so-called economic pull than any push factors.
One possible reason for this is that in reality migration
streams form a matrix among a large number of countries
with pull factors being directional and push factors
usually being nondirectional. That is, unless the
researcher is able to measure emigration in its entirety,
the sampling of a single emigration stream may not
adequately reflect the push processes at work.[45]

This general pattern also seems to hold for
population push vis-a-vis economic pull factors, the latter
demonstrating a greater number of significant t-ratios. In

---

[45] I would like to thank Dr. Lawrence Carter for
suggesting this analysis to me.

the next chapter, stage two, a multivariate analysis will
be brought to bear upon the preliminary, exploratory
analysis of the present chapter.

CHAPTER XI

FREE TRADE AND TRANS-ATLANTIC MIGRATION,

CONTINUED

Introduction

The present chapter analyses the results of stage one in the previous chapter. Here I develop multivariate models to explain migration to the U.S. on a country-by-country basis using the same dependent variables and as independent variables those which proved statistically significant in the previous chapter.

The method used for stage two was the combination into a single model, those independent variables which proved significantly correlated with migration for each country and each period: c.1828-1902; c.1828-1877; and 1877-1902. Stage two consisted of the construction of a number of multivariate models combining variables of specific categories (categorical models): U.S. variables, emigrant country economic variables, and emigrant country population variables. The independent variables which failed to retain statistical significance when entered into the appropriate categorical model were discarded. Each model was re-run after removing the variables which failed to attain t-ratios of at least 2.00 until such time that all independent variables remaining in the categorical models were statistically significant. The next step was the combination of the categorical models--U.S. variables, emigrant country population variables, and emigrant country economic variables--into a single model. The process of removing insignificant variables was repeated until a single model containing only statistically significant independent variables was attained for each period and each country. My basic goal here is to report the precise multivariate model of independent variables which correlates with each dependent variable, for each time period. I do not attempt to estimate the fit of the individual models, nor to develop predictive models. I report on which independent variables are most often revealed to be significantly associated with international migration. The significant variables' t-ratios are reported. I also determine the relative model correlations, both among countries and across time periods. Therefore, the R^2 for each model is reported. The resultant models are discussed below, country-by-country, and the models are further refined where findings seem to warrant.

A retrospective on hypotheses ten through twelve is provided following the country-by-country discussion of the findings. This retrospective is particularly concerned with the multivariate nature of stage two and with cross-period differences. The chapter closes with a general discussion of the similarities and differences of the findings ans what they suggest.

The United Kingdom, Stage Two

The findings for the United Kingdom from stage two are listed in Table 4. These findings highlight the importance of RMA and USRMA. They do not fundamentally contradict those of Thomas (1973), though Thomas concentrated on United States railway construction in the post-1870 period. What my findings suggest is that there was considerable collinearity among the independent variables. Once the process of discarding insignificant independent variables was complete, the single model into which all surviving categorical variables was merged, revealed only two significant independent variables: British railway mileage added (RMA) and U.S. railway mileage added (USRMA). This finding substantially supports Thomas (1973) who from among all independent variables in the present study, analysed only USRMA. Like Thomas, I see the railway mileage added measures as indices of economic growth.

TABLE 4

Stage Two Migration models, U.K. to U.S.

Dependent Variable: YUK

Period	Independent Variables (Lag)			R^2
1828-1902	RMA(1)	RMA(2)	RMA(4)	0.3899
	2.502*	2.914	4.492	
1828-1877	RMA(1)	RMA(2)	RMA(4)	0.5999
	2.761	2.575	5.244	
1877-1902	USRMA(0)			0.5012
	4.702			

Note: *t-ratios appear immediately below the
corresponding independent variables.

What is of particular note and gives added strength to
the findings is that no less that three lags of RMA remain
in the model for two of the three time periods.
Statistically, each lag of each variable was treated as a
separate and unrelated variable and since the two-step
transformation technique (see SAS, 1982:   187-202) removes
the effects of autocorrelation, the persistence of RMA in
three lags provides strong evidence for the inference that
RMA is an important stochastic factor, having in any given
year an impact upon emigration to the U.S. for several
subsequent years.   Another way of saying this, and what is
directly implied by Table 4, is that in a typical year,
emigration is the result (in part) of railway mileage added

for three previous years, namely the year immediately prior
to the one in question, the second year prior, and the
fourth year prior. Further evidence substantiating the
importance of RMA is the high correlation with YUK. The is
especially evident in the early time period though the high
R^2 of RMA in the early period seems to have been
replaced with as nearly a high correlation between USRMA
and YUK in the later period.

Railway mileage added, per se, probably had only
modest immediate impact upon emigration. A long-term
impact which cannot be satisfactorily measured by the time
series method is that added railway mileage in Britain may
have encouraged geographic mobility by providing more
extensive access to internal transportation. What I see
RMA as operationalizing is the general state of the
industrial sector of the British economy. My
interpretation is that, for a wide variety of individual
reasons, there existed an urge to emigrate which the income
from employment in the industrial sector provided the
wherewithall to fulfill.

Another inference may be drawn from the finding that,
for the entire period, RMA proved to be the only
significant independent variable, while in the late period
alone, USRMA proved significant. The implication is that
while RMA continued to be an important factor (though

somewhat less so, with an R^2 of 0.3899 for the entire period vis-a-vis 0.5999 for the early period), USRMA--or the pull of the industrial sector of the American economy--in the later period came to be pre-eminent, with an R^2 of 0.5012. Since the USRMA series is correlated with the YUK series in the same years (i.e. YUK does not lag USRMA), my interpretation is that the nature of USRMA is better conceptualized as the promise of industrial employment rather than as the means by which British immigrants in the U.S. financed their relatives' passages. One other point should be mentioned. I have used annual data while migration is a continuous process. If the actual causal lag is less than one year, it may be registered as a correlation at lag 0.

An alternative interpretation places USRMA on the left side of the equation, implying that migration stimulates railway construction. I cannot deny that a two-way causal relationship probably exists, but at this point I have structured the model to look at migration, alone, as a dependent variable. Even considering the possibility that immigration (or emigration) causes railway construction--for example, in the demand for rail services--I would expect USRMA to lag YUK because immigrants tended to cluster near ports of entry such as New York City or Boston.

The substantial ship traffic between British and North American ports probably provided British workers with relatively current reports of employment opportunities in the U.S. such that they could respond rapidly, especially when they had been able to save sufficient funds in past years to finance their emigration. It could also be that the decision to emigrate took less than one year to make.

The summary analysis of U.K. migration to the U.S. is that it represents, for the most part, the migration of unemployed English and Irish workers recruited from English cities.[46] The persistent influence of RMA suggests that especially in the earlier period some migrating workers, while probably facing periodic episodes of unemployment in Britain, may have been more highly skilled than the average British worker and thus better paid (and so better able to save).[47] I suggest that this category of skilled

_____

[46] See Rothstein (1975: 4). Labor recruitment abroad was an important means by which the Unites States work force was augmented. For a survey of this activity in light of federal legislation, see Immigration Commission (1911a: 375-386). Federal legislation of 1864 encouraging contract labor immigration was a clear victory for capitalism though its repeal four years later was one for labor. The Contract-Labor Law of 1885, though defective in its enforcement provisions, represented a further attempt to prevent recruitment of labor abroad.

[47] Occupational data for the first decade of this century support this suggestion. Of all immigrants admitted 1899 through 1910 who declared an occupation, over seven million total, only 20.2 percent were classified as "skilled". Among immigrants from the

workers was in such demand in the United States in the
period of American industrial expansion that it could
command sufficiently high wages to induce immigration.
What may well have been the predominant factor, the demand
for low-paid, unskilled workers, may be inferred from the
Immigration Commission's (1811b: 96) report on occupations
of immigrants in the years 1899-1910. Laborers and farm
laborers outnumbered skilled workers and professionals by a
factor of about three to one. Neither these data nor my
analysis could be said, however, to call into question the
importance of English yeoman farmers as immigrants (Hansen,
1961: 10; see also Johnson, 1913, for a study of British
emigrants to North America).

Spain, Stage Two

The findings from the analysis of Spanish migration
demonstrate both a remarkable departure from the British
findings as well as a curious similarity as seen in Table
5.

No independent variable proved statistically
significant in the early period when the analysis of stage
two reached a single, final model. The only stage one

U.K., the percentages were diverse: English, 48.7
percent; Scottish, 57.9 percent; Welsh, 56.9 percent;
but among the Irish, only 12.6 percent were skilled,
though over fifty percent were in "other occupations"
(Immigration Commission, 1911b: 96).

TABLE 5

Stage Two Migration Models, Spain to U.S.

Dependent Variable: YSPAIN

Period	Independent Variables (Lag)		R^2
1828-1902	U100(0) 4.195*	T20(0) -3.400	0.2162
1828-1877	[none]		
1877-1902	USRMA(4) 2.198		0.1736

Note: *t-ratios are placed immediately below the corresponding independent variables.

variables for the early period which attained statistical significance were USNI(0), USRMA(3), and USRMA(4). When these were combined into a single model, however, none was significant. Moreover, the correlations of those which were significant were small. This suggests that the present model is ill-suited for the analysis of Spanish emigration to the U.S., especially prior to 1877.

When the entire period was analysed, only two population variables maintained statistical significance. The t-ratio of U100 probably indicates the general inability of the largest cities,[48] themselves growing,

_____

[48] These were at mid-century, according to Chandler and Fox (1974: 96-105) Barcelonia, Madrid, Malaga, Seville, and Valencia.

to absorb national population growth, thus the positive correlation between emigration and U100.[49] Examination of the data (see Figure 7) demonstrates that U100 grew consistently while YSPAIN increased erratically. The negative correlation between YSPAIN and T20 is more complex. One indication of the complexity of the relationship is that the equation necessary to detrend the model was an eighth degree polynomial. While the overall first-degree polynomial trend (fitted visually) is clearly a straight line sloping upward with time for YSPAIN, U100, and T20 alike, a visual inspection also reveals some clear deviations from this trend for YSPAIN and T20--though not for U100. T20 (as with all population variables) is derived from a series of interpolations made between dates of enumeration or studied estimation. T20 demonstrates a smooth downward trend from 1830 to 1857 at which point the trend reverses and continues upward for the remainder of the series reaching a final point somewhat higher than its starting datum. YSPAIN takes what would best be described as an exponential curve upward from 1829 until the mid-1850s, decidedly contrary to T20 but in the same direction as U100. From that point, until a trough is

---

[49] Spain may have grown by as much as fifty percent in the first half of the ninteenth century: from ten or eleven million to about fifteen million (Kiernan, 1966: 18-19).

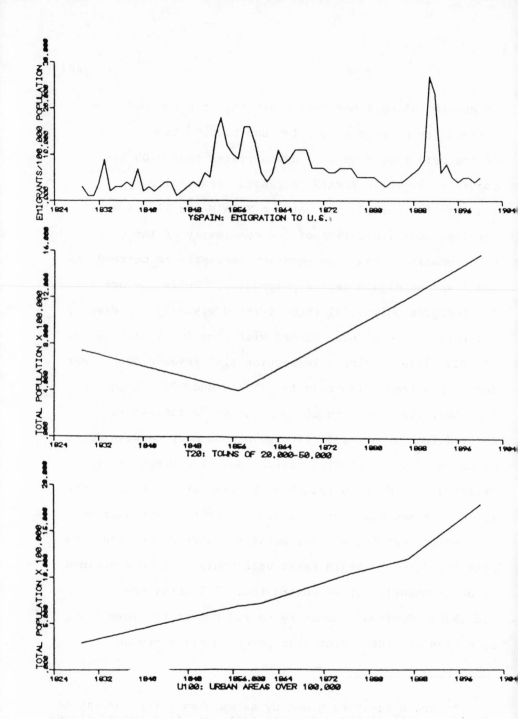

FIGURE 7:   YSPAIN, T20, and U100

reached in 1883, the trend of YSPAIN is downward, contrary
to both U100 and T20. Between 1883 and 1902, most YSPAIN
data demonstrate a gentle upward trend except for 1891,
1892, and 1902 which are markedly higher than neighboring
data. Thus the post-1883 trend is in a similar direction
for YUK, U100, and T20.

The substantive interpretation of YSPAIN, U100, and
T20 is that the generalized environmental crisis
(exacerbated by the persistence of feudal agriculture)[50]
and the mid-century period of revolution (see Kiernan,
1966 or Marx and Engels, 1939) contributed to a
depopulation of towns of 20,000 to 50,000 and a rise in
emigration which appeared in U.S. immigration statistics in
the mid-1850s. From that point onward, while there is a
general increase in the rate of migration, similar to the
increase in urban and town populations, there are the
spikes in migration in the 1880s and 1902 related possibly
to economic crises in Spain. The increasing trends just
noted, I would say, are related to a single phenomenon my
data cannot operationalize: latent reserve army migration.

The statistical significance of USRMA, particularly as
it appears in the fourth lag (the effect on YSPAIN is felt
four years after it is recorded in USRMA), is suggestive of

---

[50] "In over-populated Galicia extreme sub-division of
holdings was driving thousands to emigrate to America"
(Kiernan, 1966: 22).

a point made in the last chapter for lagged positive
correlations with economic variables. I suggested that
immigrants to the U.S. were able to finance the immigration
of their relatives still in Europe according to the state
of their own finances, itself dependent upon the health of
the American economy as measured, for example, by USRMA.
The fourth lag suggests that Spain was somewhat outside the
center of international commerce and economy[51] and that
knowledge of American economic conditions simply took a
great time longer to reach Spanish workers than it did to
reach English or Irish workers. Available data do not
allow for a definitive determination of whether the key
factor was remittances from the U.S. to Spain or the
knowledge by Spanish workers of conditions in the United
States.

In summary, the lack of significant independent
variables in the first period and the low R^2s for the
other models, call into serious question the
appropriatenes, for the Spanish case, of the independent
variables utilized here. As was suggested in the last
chapter, the attempt to develop a measure suggestive of
emigration by the latent reserve army or other population
changes in rural areas was largely unsuccessful. Had I

---

[51] Hobsbawm (1977: 221) specifically excludes Iberian
states from those which were members of the world's
emerging industrialzed sector as of mid-century.

been able to do so, I would guess that such a variable would contribute rather more to explaining the Spanish case.

The Netherlands, Stage Two

The stage two findings on Dutch migration to the United States demonstrate considerable similarity to the findings on British migration though, as demonstrated in Table 6, there are some minor but important differences. The major similarities are that RMA and USRMA are the only variables which maintain significance in, respectively, the early period and the late period for both YUK and YHOLLAND. While it is true that RMA for YHOLLAND is a less striking finding with a smaller R^2 and only a single significant lag, the findings are intepreted similarly to those of the U.K. For the early period, the income provided in the industrial sector of the Dutch economy (measured by RMA) is seen as having been sufficient to provide travel funds for those inclined to emigrate. For the late period, the promise of industrial employment in the U.S. (measured by USRMA) is interpreted as having provided motivation for potential Dutch emigrants. The Netherlands, a leading maritime nation, would likely have general access to current knowledge about the state of the American economy provided by sailors and merchants returning from voyages abroad.

TABLE 6

Stage Two Migration Models, Netherlands to U.S.

Dependent Variable: YHOLLAND

Period	Independent Variables (Lag)			R^2
1828-1902	USRMA(0) 2.991*	USIMPORT(0) 4.559	USIMPORT(2) -2.985	0.4384
1828-1877	RMA(1) 3.325			0.1972
1877-1902	USRMA 3.344			0.3370

Note: *t-ratios appear immediately below the corresponding independent variables.

The main difference is found in the data for the entire period. For British migrants, the significant measure is a U.K. variable, RMA. For the Dutch migrants, the significant measure is a combination of U.S. variables: USRMA and USIMPORT.[52] These findings suggest that the

---

[52] The best explanation I have for the presence of the negative correlation of the second lag of USIMPORT is posed in the previous chapter. There I suggested that some immigrants (older, middle-class) may have delayed sending remittances to finance the voyage of their families until such time that enough money was saved that the entire family could be admitted together. I am not convinced that this is a particularly strong argument. With USIMPORT(2) removed and YHOLLAND regressed on USRMA(0) and USIMPORT(0) both remain significant and produce an R^2 of 0.3686. This suggests that the second (negative) lag of USIMPORT, regardless of how it may be explained, is not particularly important as the R^2 drops only slightly when it is removed. This is what I would expect.

"pull" of the industrial sector of the U.S. economy was felt in The Netherlands sooner than in the United Kingdom--probably well before 1877. This would seem to mean that the British industrial sector (measured by railway mileage added) was more robust than that of the Netherlands, yielding to the growing American economy at a later date than did the Dutch economy. For a less robust economy in a country of emigration, it should not be unexpected that economic pull factors should come into play sooner than for a more robust economy of emigrants.

Switzerland, Stage Two

Table 7 suggests that some important change took place in the context of Swiss migration to the United States over the period 1828 to 1902. The best evidence of this is the lack of a significant independent variable in stage two for the early period. Both the entire period and the late period, analysed separately, maintained more than one significant independent variable, including one which was identical: USIMPORT(0).

What is particularly interesting is the finding of no significantly correlated independent variables in the pre-1877 period vis-a-vis four in the post-1877 period with a high correlation between these and YSWISS. The moderate correlation of USRMA(1) and USIMPORT(0) with YSWISS for the entire period suggests that the "pull" of the American

TABLE 7

Stage Two Migration Models, Switzerland to U.S.

Dependent Variable: YSWISS

Period	Independent Variables (Lag)				R^2
1828-1902	USRMA(1) 3.746*	USIMPORT(0) 2.333			0.3290
1828-1877	[none]				
1877-1902	USIMPEXP(4) -6.036	USIMPORT(0) 3.194	USRMA(0) 4.532	USRMA(2) 5.438	0.9022

Note: *t-ratios appear immediately below the corresponding independent variables.

economy became increasingly more important, as the economy grew and prospered, when this finding is compared with the pre-1877 and post-1877 findings.

One of the most puzzling models in stage two was that which provided a very high R^2 for the post-1877 period but which contained an important negative correlation with USIMPEXP(4). Suspecting that USIMPEXP(4) was responsible for relatively little of the correlation, I ran a regression on the model without USIMPEXP(4) finding that the statistical significance of USIMPORT was reduced to a t-ratio of less than 2.00. Removing USIMPORT(0) from the model left USRMA(0) and USRMA(2) with significant t-ratios (3.915 and 3.328 respectively) but reduced the model's

R^2 from 0.9022 (as displayed in Table 7) to 0.5034, a marked drop for which my previously stated explanation regarding the withholding of remittances seems less than satisfactory. What it would seem to represent is a high collinearity between USIMPEXP(4) and USIMPORT(0) vis-a-vis the USRMA series. The lower R^2 is probably more realistic.

France, Stage Two

The findings on French migration to the U.S. are somewhat inconsistent when the correlations of Table 8 are examined. The inconsistency is found mainly in the early, pre-1877 period. Here we find we find the third lag of IMPORTS negatively correlated with YFRANCE and the fourth lag positively correlated.

I would like to attribute the negativity of IMPORTS(3) for the entire period to a reluctance on the part of the French to emigrate in relatively good economic times (as measured by IMPORTS). However, the three year lag makes that a dubious proposition. The fact that IMPORTS(4) is positively correlated to YFRANCE makes the explanation even more untenable. I simply have no appealing hypothesis to explain the inconsistencies; I would only point out the relatively tiny R^2 and assume that whatever factor is responsible is also relatively unimportant. What

TABLE 8

Stage Two Migration Models, France to U.S.

Dependent Variable: YFRANCE

Period	Independent Variables (Lag)		R^2
1828-1902	IMPORTS(3)		0.0667
	-2.237*		
1828-1877	IMPORTS(3)	IMPORTS(4)	0.1825
	-3.134	2.956	
1877-1902	C50(0)	USRMA(0)	0.8217
	-7.843	2.977	

Note: *t-ratios appear immediately below the corresponding independent variables.

complicates the analysis of French immigration to the U.S., but what may explain the findings which cover periods before 1877, is that France was a net labor importing country, especially of Belgians and Italians (Brogan, 1967: 417). In Ravenstein's (1889) analysis, he found that countries such as France, with vast, relatively under-populated agricultural regions, tended to be countries of net immigration. This situation of net immigration took place in the context of a low birth rate for France and a declining rural population (see Brogan, 1967: 406ff; Thomson, 1968: 9-10). I would tend to attribute the general situation of relative population stagnation in France vis-a-vis most other developing

capitalist countries to the failure of industrial
capitalism to take firm hold there as it did, for example,
in England or Germany. On the issue of political and
economic development in eighteenth century France, see
Marx's (1973) Class Struggles in France and The Eighteenth
Brumaire of Louis Bonaparte.

The post-1877 period findings are more interesting.
We see the familiar pattern of USRMA suggesting that the
American economy tended to attract French immigrants as
well as other nationalities. But of greater note is the
correlation of C50 with YFRANCE. Not only is the t-ratio
quite high but when C50 is removed from the model, the
R^2 drops from 0.8217 to 0.2088; with C50 alone, the
R^2 is 0.7092. This is highly suggestive of an
important relationship between C50 and French migration to
the United States. A visual inspection of the data (see
Figure 8) reinforces the statistical findings even though
the statistical findings involve the stochastic
relationship while the visual analysis is of trend. The
visual analysis (which follows) generally tends to discount
the possibility of a readily identifiable spurious factor
as is suggested below in the context of YBELGIUM.

C50 for France seems to operate similarly to T20 for
Spain. C50 falls from 1881 to 1891 indicating a drop in
the population of cities in the 50,000 to 100,000 range

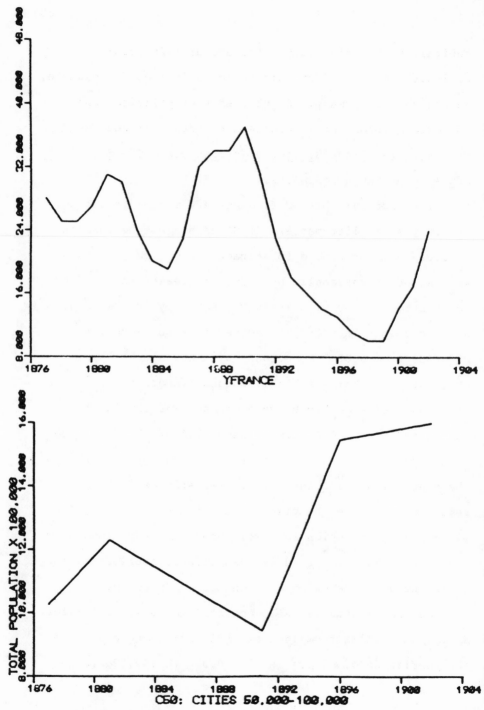

FIGURE 8:   YFRANCE and C50, 1877-1902

while YFRANCE rises somewhat. This would seem to suggest
that the source of at least part of the emigration to the
U.S. was from cities of that size range. After 1891, C50
rises, suggesting an economic change which allows cities of
that size to absorb population. YFRANCE drops consistently
from 1891 to 1899, then reverses. This suggests that for
the 1890s, potential French emigrants to the U.S. stayed
in, or migrated to French cities of 50,000 to 100,000.
These data do not give a clear indication of the social
class makeup of the French migrants to the U.S. It would
seem to suggest a disproportionate middle-class component
among French migrants to the United States. This is borne
out by the U.S. Immigration Commission's (1911b: 96)
findings for the period 1899-1910 that among the French
migrants, 9.3 percent were in professional occupations
while only 1.4 percent of all immigrants to the U.S. were
professionals.

Belgium, Stage Two

Belgian migration to the United States presents
another unusual finding. As Table 9 demonstrates, U.S.
population density seems to be correlated with YBELGIUM
both negatively and positively in respectively lags two and
three. This holds for both the pre-1877 period and the
entire period. However, since no reasonable substantive

explanation for this has presented itself, I suspected that there may be an anomoly in the data.

TABLE 9

Stage Two Migration Models, Belgium to U.S.

Dependent Variable: YBELGIUM

Period	Independent Variables (Lag)			R^2
1828-1902	USPD(2) -3.488*	USPD(3) 5.281		0.3570
1830-1877	USRMA(0) 3.454	USPD(2) -4.140	USPD(3) 4.859	0.5201
1877-1902	T20(1) 2.843			0.2601

Note: *t-ratios appear immediately below the corresponding independent variables.

A visual examination of USPD(2) and USPD(3) vis-a-vis YBELGIUM lends support to the idea that the correlation may be spurious notwithstanding the significant t-ratios. This is supported by the nature of USPD which, like other population variables, consists of a series of interpolated values between years of census enumeration, altered by several increases in the area of the United States. This presented a situation in which usually the USPD(3) datum for a given year was slightly less than USPD(2) since the general trend was increasing. However, whenever the

population density dropped due to an increase in the size
of U.S. national territory, USPD(3), lagging USPD(2) by one
year, registered a higher value than USPD(2). The data
series demonstrate this in 1847, 1850, and 1869. Upon
examining YBELGIUM, I found unusually high values in 1847,
1850, 1856, 1866, and 1869. There followed a trough in
1877, a sharp increase to peak in 1892, a sharp drop to
1897, and then another sharp increase. I hypothesized that
the spikes of 1847, 1850, and 1869, working in concert with
the downward trend between 1892 and 1897, were responsible
for the correlations with both USPD(2) and USPD(3). By
manipulating the values of YBELGIUM for 1847, 1850, and
1869--reducing them to approximately the same amplitude as
their neighboring years--and re-running the models
portrayed in Table 9, USPD(2) and USPD(3) were no longer
statistically significant. I then removed USPD (all lags)
from the analysis and found no independent variable
stastically significant for the entire period. USRMA
remained statistically significant for the pre-1877 period
with a t-ratio of 3.630 and an R^2 of 0.2304. The
findings for the post-1877 period were not changed. My
removal of statistically significant independent variables
from the models requires further discussion.

In the 1840s, the United States population density
underwent a marked drop with the acquisition of additional,

sparsely populated territory. At about the same time,
Belgium underwent a period of crisis, second "only in terms
of actual suffering" to Ireland due to political conflicts
and failed harvests (Hobsbawm, 1977: 368-370). These
problems were accompanied by high levels of industrial
unemployment and Flemish migration to France. The high
rate of Belgian migration to the United States from 1847 to
1850 would seem to reflect the increase in the "floating
reserve army" for reasons not easily operationalized in a
time series analysis. This exodus from Belgium is
conceptualized as a "random shock" to the YBELGIUM series.

The presence of a modest correlation between YBELGIUM
and T20(1) suggests that Belgian towns of 20,000 to 50,000
could not grow fast enough to absorb the latent reserve
population of the countryside thus emigration to the U.S.
represented one viable option for some of the peasants.

Denmark, Stage two

The final migration stream analysed was that from
Denmark. Table 10 demonstrates a number of patterns which
should by now be familiar.

The importance of USRMA in its various lags has been
stressed repeatedly in the analysis of previous models.
All but one variable which maintained statistical
significance through the stage two analysis was a U.S.

TABLE 10

Stage Two Migration Models, Denmark to U.S.

Dependent Variable: YDENMARK

Period	Independent Variables (Lag)				R^2
1828-1902	USRMA(0)	USRMA(2)	USRMA(4)		0.5682
	6.235*	5.297	4.655		
1828-1877	U100(2)	USNI(0)	USIMPORT(2)	USIMPORT(4)	0.8886
	6.060	-7.185	6.759	-3.750	
1877-1902	USIMPEXP(4)	USIMPORT(0)	USRMA(0)	USRMA(2)	
	-6.676	5.297	5.632	5.729	
	USRMA(4)				0.9408
	5.089				

Note: *t-ratios appear immediately below the
corresponding independent variables.

variable and this presents a strong case for the economic
"pull" interpretation. The single Danish variable, U100(2)
in the pre-1877 period, indicates that Copenhagan's
industrial sector, at least in the middle of the nineteenth
century, did not develop as fast as did the surplus of
workers from smaller towns and rural areas. The absense of
any "economic push" variables helps confirm this.

Taking a closer look at the U.S. variables, we find
three with the unexpected but now familiar negative
correlations. The negative correlations between migration
rate and the U.S. trade variables have been tentatively

explained by the mover/stayer approach or by the posibility
of a tendency of some immigrants to withhold remittances
until the entire family could join them in the United
States. The same is to be said for the negative
correlation with USNI. At present, I have no means of
verifying this speculation.

It would seem illogical to think that a thriving U.S.
economy would repel immigrants and a stagnant economy
attract them. Aside from the delayed remittances
hypothesis, about the only other way the negative
correlations could be explained is to suggest that the
Danish economy (for example) experienced simultaneous, but
more severe episodes of economic crisis such that migrants
fled from worse to bad economic conditions. There is
little evidence for this. Another possibility is that
Danish emigration was random, though such an analysis is
not in keeping with the assumptions underlying this study.
In stage two, in the development of categorical models, no
Danish economic variable remained statistically significant
for the entire period. This tends to discount the
explanation for the negative USNI and USIMPORT(4) for that
period. For the post-1877 period, however, the Danish
economy categorical model consisted solely of RMA(2) with a
t-ratio of -2.744 and an R^2 of 0.2466. This does seem
to suggest that the Danes tended to emigrate to the the

United States during bad times but remain at home during good times. Unfortunately, RMA(2) and USIMPEXP(4) are not correlated. This does not support such a hypothesis.

If one were to assume that the negative correlations of the U.S. variables with YDENMARK were relatively unimportant and remove them from the models, the assumption would be proved wrong. For the pre-1877 period, with the negatively correlated independents removed, the model was re-run with the loss of significance of U100(2), leaving only USIMPORT(2). The correlation between YDENMARK and USIMPORT(2), alone, R^2 drops to a mere 0.2979. There is clearly a process at work which the existing data cannot fully explain.

Retrospective on Hypotheses Ten through Twelve

There were insufficient data available to confirm or falsify the hypotheses posed in chapter ten. This was due to limitations inherent in the original collection of immigration data and/or in the data set from which the population and economic data were derived. Because of the unavailability of suitable data series for all countries of the Atlantic economy, I will not pose my findings in such a way that inappropriate generalizations to the larger population might be made. I will not analyse these hypotheses in the context of attempting to reject a null hypothesis. However, I will indicate whether the findings demonstrate patterns which tend to support the hypotheses, or not.

Hypothesis ten concerned economic factors. The findings upon which the following discussion is based are to be found in the first row (period: c.1828-1902) of Table 4 through Table 10. I would expect to find evidence of an "economic push" from countries already undergoing industrialization as an indication of the presence of a "floating reserve army" emigrating to the U.S. The findings would seem to bear this out.

For the United Kingdom, the only variable which maintained significance in stage two for the entire period was Railway Mileage Added (RMA). With an R^2 of about 0.4, this is evidence for the operation of a floating reserve army emigrating to the U.S. The only other country with a similar finding was France with an unremarkable correlation ($R^2=0.0667$) between YFRANCE and an economic push variable (IMPORTS). Three other countries--Switzerland, Denmark, and The Netherlands--had economic pull factors in evidence suggesting either latent or floating reserve emigration, with the decisive factor being the state of the U.S. economy. Spain demonstrated a population push while the findings for Belgium were inconclusive.

Hypothesis eleven addresses rural emigration in the late feudal, early industrial capitalist countries of Europe. Here, analysis is based upon findings reported in rows one (c.1828-1902) and two (c.1828-1877) of Table 4 through Table 10. What I looked for were findings that R20 was correlated with the rate of emigration. This would indicate a relationship between changes in the population of rural areas and emigration. It is far from a perfect measure (as I have suggested), but it is the best measure to be developed from the data at hand.

Nowhere did R20 withstand the stage two analysis. Turning back to stage one, however, Belgium, Denmark, The Netherlands, and the United Kingdom demonstrated some preliminary association. I must conclude that R20 was an insufficiently precise measure of rural population change. I therefore am unable to report any satisfactory findings for hypothesis eleven, either for or against.

Hypothesis twelve is the last one. This hypothesis suggests an important change in the world economy taking place in the 1870s. It suggests that changes in international migration should correspond to the theoretical change from the industrial stage of capitalism to the imperialist stage. Since the key feature of imperialism as related to migration was the export of capital from the more developed to the lesser developed

captialist countries, I would look for evidence of a shift
to economic pull factors in the later period. In addition,
I would look for a diminishing of population push factors
in the later period. The findings analysed for hypothesis
twelve are reported in rows two and three of Table 4
through Table 10.

The findings for the United Kingdom met with
expectations. There were no population push variables in
evidence at the end of stage two. There was a marked shift
from economic push to economic pull factors: from RMA in
the early period to USRMA in the late period. Similarly,
The Netherlands also saw the same shift with the same
variables though the R^2 was only half to two-thirds
that of the U.K. This should not be unexpected since the
U.K. was more advanced at that conjuncture and economic
variables would be expected to have greater impact.

The remaining countries were less clearly supportive
of the hypothesis. While France also demonstrated a shift
from economic push (IMPORTS) to economic pull (USRMA), a
population push variable also appeared for the first time
in stage two in the late period. Denmark demonstrated a
fairly consistent series of economic pull variables in both
periods with the falling out of a population push variable
after the early period. Such a finding would not be
inconsistent with the hypothesis in that it suggests that

capitalist economic development within Denmark was far less influencial than the American economy.

For Switzerland, there was no significant independent variable for the early period though a series of economic pull variables attained a fairly high correlation (R^2=0.9) in the late period. This is also consistent with the hypothesis though, frankly, I find the substantial difference between the two periods somewhat troubling. I would not have expected such a marked change. In some ways, a similar situation is demonstrated in the findings on Spain. Like Switzerland, there was no variable which attained significance in the early period while an economic pull variable was correlated with emigration in the late period. Unlike Switzerland, the R^2 (0.1736) was much smaller. Another point of interest is that Spain and Switzerland were probably the least developed countries of those in the analysis as of the early period and this may account for the early period findings.

Findings from Belgium were the only ones which seemed to contradict the hypothesis. Disregarding the USPD variable (as discussed above), an economic pull variable (USRMA) appeared in the early period while a population push variable (T20) appeared in the late period. The Belgium findings notwithstanding, the bulk of the evidence tends to support hypothesis twelve.

Conclusion

Of the three hypothesis (ten through twelve) addressed in this and the previous chapter, ten and twelve seemed to receive general support while eleven was inconclusive. Hypothesis ten suggested that the floating reserve army would be an important component of emigration from the industrializing countries to the U.S. Hypothesis eleven suggested that in the late feudal, early industrial countries of Europe, latent reserve migration would be an important component subject, however, to environmental interventions. My inability to formulate a satisfactory measure of the reserve army on the basis of the available data, however, has made analysis of hypothesis eleven problematical. Hypothesis twelve suggested that changes in international migration would correspond to structural changes in the world captialist economy as the industrial stage gave way to the imperialist stage. This is largely supported by the evidence.

There are several important summary findings of stage two. I found that United States economic variables, especially railway mileage added, were important explanatory factors in the analysis of immigration from the U.K., Spain, The Netherlands, Switzerland, France, Belgium, and Denmark. The impact of the U.S. "economic pull" seemed to have been felt much more strongly in the later period, after 1877. The importance of the later period, representing the imperialist stage of capitalist development, is underscored by the relative consistency of findings across countries. My best explanation is that greater amounts of capital were exported from the industrial center of the Atlantic economy (especially England) to be invested in less advanced capitalist countries. These flows of capital helped stimulate a number of national economies, most especially as demonstrated here, that of the United States. The demographic variables seemed to be of least importance. One reason for this, I believe, was my inability to develop a measure of the latent reserve army migration (or rural population change) on the basis of available data. Had this been possible, I would speculate that a fairly substantial portion of the migration would have been explained.

Perhaps the most surprising finding was a persistent negative correlation between some lagged U.S. economic variables and the migration measures. One possible reason was that "movers" and "stayers" are influenced by different factors and at different times. I also suggested that it may be due to a tendency of some immigrants to withhold remitting their savings to finance the immigration of their families until sufficient funds were available to allow all members to emigrate. Frankly, I do not find this explanation particularly convincing, especially in those cases where the negative correlation was substantial.

CHAPTER XII

CONCLUSION

Goals of the Study

The immediate goal of this study was to effect a joining of two different theoretical perspectives in order to propose a means by which migration could by analysed in historical perspective. A better understanding of international labor migration is the long-term goal of the present work. International labor migration, in the capitalist epoch, has helped bring together labor and capital resulting in economic growth far greater than ever before experienced. But it has also contributed to the vastly uneven development of national economies such that tremendous and serious international conflicts have emerged. International labor migration has also contributed to various political, economic, and demographic problems in both countries of emigration and immigration—though it seems to have helped mitigate problems of labor shortage or unemployment in some areas.

The theoretical perspectives articulated in this thesis are the homeostatic model as developed by Wrigley (1969) and the Marxian perspective. Wrigley's model was designed to explain the historical demography of population growth, especially the interaction of fertility and mortality. Marx's theory was designed to critique the capitalist mode of production. Both theoretical perspectives address migration peripherally but I have attempted to bring migration to the center of the analysis, as the focal point where the two theories are joined. This took place in chapters two, three, and four. At the end of chapter four, I proposed a series of hypotheses suggested by Marxist historical materialism viewed in light of the homeostatic model. To conclude the study, I review these hypotheses, evaluate the theoretical potential developed, and suggest a few directions for future research.

Hypotheses Reviewed

The first hypothesis concerned the analysis of peasant migration at the height of European feudalism. I suggested that colonial migration resulted from long-term environmental changes which tended to allow for an increase in population without accompanying social structrual adaptation. Migration was seen as the demographic means by which feudal communities adapted to the tendency of their populations to increase. The particular type of migration--colonizing or conquering--was hypothesized as being related to the particulars of peasant subjugation. Feudalism was characterized by a political bondage of serf to lord and an economic bondage of serf to land, the latter mediated by the former. Where the political bond was predominant, I suggested that conquest migration was the primary form of migration. Where the economic bond was predominant, I suggested that colonial migration was the primary form.

The homeostatic model helped to locate migration within the complex of demographic, socio-economic, and environmental factors. The Marxian historical periodization suggested specific social structural factors which revealed essential differences in the types of migration response. The Marxian perspective also suggested economic reasons for the differences.

The second hypothesis concerned the fourteenth century population crisis. I suggested that the period of population increase in the centuries prior to the fourteenth tended to drive the actual population size toward the upper limits of the homeostatic carrying capacity. Without out-migration from growing communities, the population pressure came to be exerted on the social system of feudalism. But I was mainly interested in the

phenomenon of corporate migration. Corporate migration
served to relieve the immediate pressure of population upon
specific communities by the out-migration and colonization
of new territories. The problem with this tactic, however,
was that such colonial resettlement migration was sponsored
by established feudal lords thus extending their
geographical reach, but weakening their political hold as
the primary moment of peasant colonial subjugation was the
economic--the bondage of serf to land.

This extension of cultivation and weakening of the
political bond of serf to lord was not able to withstand
the systemic shocks wrought by the Black Death and other
episodes of population retrogression in the fourteenth and
subsequent centuries. While it may be true that migration
in the post-fourteenth century period accompanied the
downfall of feudalism, my hypothesis was that colonial
migration in the period prior to the population crisis was
the main demographic contributing factor. Of course, the
colonial migration was, itself, a product of the social
structure.

In the wake of the population crisis and its impact on
the feudal social structure, my third hypothesis suggests
that structural changes took place such that population
homeostasis was established at a relatively temporary
lower, post-crisis level. That is to say, the subtle

social changes which accompanied the eleventh through thirteenth century colonial migration movement were assaulted by the population retrogression of the fourteenth century such that the social system which emerged from the crisis could no longer support as large a population as had been supported before the Black Death. Of course, continued episodes of pestilence and war helped to keep the numbers down, but the actual population size must be separated conceptually from homeostasis—the theoretical carrying capacity of the social and environmental system.

The crisis period of negative population growth and the post-crisis period of slow and intermitant recovery has been characterized as "population stagnation." Hypothesis four suggests that this lower population size was maintained not only by continued high mortality but, especially, by changes in cultural practices. While mortality helped to keep the actual population size at a low post-crisis level, it was assisted by lower fertility resulting from changes in household composition which, in addition, reflected the lower level of population homeostasis.

In the centuries which followed the population crisis, two tendencies emerged which countered the tendency toward stagnation. One was the slow recovery of population in the face of environmental constraints and the other was further structural change which reversed the lower, post-crisis homestasis allowing for a substantial increase in the population carrying capacity.

Hypothesis five suggests that the actual population increase associated with the recovery from population stagnation contributed to the sixteenth century price revolution in two ways. For one, demand-pull inflation emerged in the agricultural sector of late feudal society, as the period of stagnation passed. For the other, the second colonial period--the period of American colonization--was accompanied by the importation of specie which is said to have helped fuel inflation. While these explanations are not new, they are formulated here for the first time in the context of the homeostatic model, with a special focus on migration.

Hypothesis six takes up the homeostatic element of the recovery from the population stagnation. The differential between the modestly increasing size of the actual population and the more rapidly increasing homeostasis is addressed. Certain environmental factors, especially pestilence and weather-related crop failures, contributed to high mortality which continued to constrain population growth. However, economic change related to the downfall of feudalism and the emergence of capitalism contributed to a greatly increased population carrying capacity. The situation, I hypothesized, was that the slow recovery from the fourteenth century crisis, coupled with important and fundamental economic changes taking place, established a situation in which the actual population size approached ever nearer the lower limits of the rising population carrying capacity of late feudal Europe.

Hypothesis seven concerns the latent upward pressure on actual population size exerted by the increasing homeostasis. The key to this hypothesis is the period of urbanization, caused in no small part by rural structural changes which appeared demographically as peasant migration resulting from the enclosure movement. Another aspect of urbanization which affected the differential between actual population size and homeostasis was the tendency for cities to actively attract in-migrants because some urban areas could not maintain their sizes in accord with economic needs by natural increase alone. The demographic effect of this was the redistribution of population from rural areas where fertility was increasing to urban areas where the mortality rate was much higher. This redistribution is hypothesized as having restrained population recovery at the national level.

Urban social changes may also have been associated with consumption. The increased consumption of products in the process of production by petty commodity producers,

rather than at the end of a production-consumption cycle by
the ruling class, is suggested as being partially
responsible for the emergence of the merchant and artisan
classes of nascent capitalism. The migration of serfs to
the cities, among other things, while it may have delayed
national population recovery, also contributed to the
development of both classes necessary for capitalism--the
bourgoisie and the working class.

Hypothesis eight is an attempt to explain the
demographic transition in homeostatic terms. The general
tendency for population recovery to take place in the
context of more rapidly increasing homeostasis helps
establish a model which may explain the period of rapid
population increase seen at the beginning of the capitalist
mode of production. One generally accepted hypothesis is
that mortality rates fell, and this is clearly a key
factor. What I want to stress, however, is the interaction
of the environmental and social structural components of
the homeostatic model. The mortality change I attributed
to environmental changes which reduced the virulence of the
agents causing plague and to economic progress which
allowed for the transportation and storage of foodstuffs to
counter starvation in some cities. The reason population
could grow to such heights once some of the causes of
mortality were mitigated without meeting with Malthusian

disaster is that social structural changes--particularly
those which took place in the cities. Changes in the mode
of production had established a population carrying
capacity able to absorb numbers which once would likely
have destroyed the system.

The foregoing analysis has served mainly to
demonstrate the potential of the problematic for bringing
migration more to the center of attention. By so doing,
the role of migration in the historical process of feudal
dissolution in Europe is better understood. The following
hypotheses attempt to extend the analysis to international
migration.

Hypothesis nine addressed the period of overseas
colonization. I suggested that the social systems of the
Americas were not well suited for protocapitalist
production which was developing in Britain and other parts
of Europe. Moreover, the workforce needed could not be
recruited in Europe by traditional feudal means as the
feudal system had come into complete disarray. The forced
migration of laborers to the Americas was based upon
Iberian slavery and British indentured servitude. This was
the case at least until the full development of industrial
capitalism in the nineteenth century when free
international labor migration came to predominate.

With regard to the homeostatic model, I suggested that in this period, economic factors were the most important determinants of demographic change. With the passing of the plague and the increasingly rapid population growth, the onus for controlling the population problem was passed to the social structure, particularly the political economy of mercantilism.

A final, and important, feature of hypothesis nine was the suggestion that the geographical loci of capitalist development in the Americas was determined in large part by the type of labor migration and associated organization of production which was superimposed upon the American territories. My hypothesis was that capitalism developed most vigorously in the northeastern region of the U.S. which had been spared the legacy of slavery and which had received large numbers of petty producers as immigrants.

The availability of quantitative data allow for a somewhat different treatment of the final three hypotheses. Hypothesis ten concerned migration of industrial workers. In this hypothesis I suggested that among industrialized (or industrializing) countries of Europe, the state of the national economy of the country of emigration would exercise an important influence upon migration to the U.S. My findings gave support to this hypothesis.

Hypothesis ten concerned the latent reserve army and emigration to the United States. Unfortunately, the best measure of the latent reserve which I could derive from the data set did not support the hypothesis. My preliminary analysis of the variables indicated that the variable in question (R20), in fact did not measure the rural population as it was intended. For that reason, I must declare the results of the analysis of hypothesis eleven as inconclusive until such time that a more fitting variable can be developed.

The final hypothesis, number twelve, addressed the problem of the transformation of the capitalist system from the industrial stage to the imperialist stage. I suggested that if, indeed, such a major change took place in the world economy, evidence for it should be found in international migration. My findings, for the most part, supported this hypothesis. For six of seven countries a tendency toward greater influence of the United States economy upon international migration was found. The importance of this is that in the imperialist stage, capital was exported from the most advanced countries (e.g. the U.K.) for investment in such growing economies as the United States. The greater influence of the American economy upon emigration from Europe is interpreted as a reflection of the imperialist system.

Theoretical Potential of Marxism Merged with the Homeostatic Model

It was not the intent of this study to present a new and fully developed theory of international migration. I had found certain deficiencies in the various theories which purported to provide the framework for the analysis of migration and attempted, simply, to provide a somewhat eclectic but internally consistent articulation of the more promising aspects of existing theories which addresed migration. The result was a merging of certain aspects of the homeostatic model with a Marxian historical periodization.

The perspective utilized here represents the first, and admittedly tentative, step in the development of a new theory of international migration. It is not a theory in itself, but I beleive it has demonstrated certain potential worthy of critique and further development. I believe that the theories as articulated here are fundamentally consistent with one another and jointly better explain population phenomena than does either constituent theory alone.

For the moment, my task is completed. What the theoretical content of this study demands, first of all, is sound critique--both from proponents of the Marxian perspective and from historical demographers. Secondly, should the theoretical perspective under development here survive such a critique (perhaps in amended form), it needs to be applied to the problems of migration and historical demography from different directions than are represented here.

Directions for Future Research

My study has focussed on what at each conjuncture in question was the leading national economy, at least as I saw it. Essentially, this meant a focus on England which began to shift to the United States in the two chapters prior to the present. Future research in the pre-capitalist period might profitably be focussed on German migration and economic development. More direct attention to Iberia might also be made, especially in comparison to Germany or Britain.

One key demographic issue which requires further attention is the precise means by which population was allowed to recover from the fourteenth century population crisis, in light of continued adverse environmental factors. What, exactly, was the social structural change which reversed the lower homeostasis in the immediate post-crisis period? What was the immediate change which allowed population to increase? Did environmental factors gradually diminish or did economic reorganization (even in the dying days of feudalism) begin to allow for the

survival of larger numbers in the face of continued
environmental onslaught?

Another major area of research which time limitations
have prevented me from addressing here is international
migration in the twentieth century. Theoretically, the key
problems for me were the periods of transition: from
feudalism to capitalism and, within the capitalist system,
from the industrial stage to the imperialist stage. We
need to know whether the patterns of migration discerned
under the period of free trade are also to be found in the
twentieth century. If so, then the question becomes: is
the historical model which I have begun to develop here
also applicable to the post-World War Two period of
international migration? An important consideration here
is the shift from East-West migration (Europe to the
Americas) to North-South (Africa to Europe, within Europe,
and within the Americas.)

I believe the potential exists for the application of
the homeostatic model (as adapted here) to modern problems
of international labor migration. Should such analysis
hold forth, certain policy implications my also be implied.
The single greatest implication I would foresee would be
the need to relieve the economic inequality within the
world economy and within the class structures of the
capitalist nations of the world.

Finally, a word should be said about the limitations of such a study. The most striking limitation was in the availability and quality of data. While the migration series were precise, they were open to some degree of error. One must assume that whatever errors there were, were not systematic. Much the same might be said about the economic data. The population data, however, present another problem. Not only were the censuses (sources of the population data) limited in accuracy, but numerous interpolations were made between census records. One of the most important empirical tasks for the future is the reconstruction of historical demographic data, a task which has only just begun.

BIBLIOGRAPHY

Abramovitz, Moses. 1964. Evidences of Long Swings in
Aggregate Construction Since the Civil War. New York:
National Bureau of Economic Research, Columbia
University Press.

_____. 1968. "The Passing of the Kuznets Cycle."
Economica (November): 349-367.

Abrams, Philip. 1982. Historical Sociology. Ithaca:
Cornell University Press.

_____, and E.A. Wrigley, Ed. 1978. Towns in Society:
Essays in Economic History and Historical Sociology.
Cambridge: Cambridge University Press.

Adelman, Irma. 1965. "Long Cycles--Fact or Artifact?"
American Economic Review (June): 444-463.

Amin, Samir. 1976. Unequal Development. New York:
Monthly Review Press.

Anderson, Perry. 1974. Lineages of the Absolutist State.
London: NLB.

Ashton, T.S. 1955. An Economic History of England: The
18th Century. London: Methuen and Co. Ltd.

Babbie, Earl. 1979. The Practice of Social Research.
Second edition. Belmont, California: Wadsworth
Publishing Co.

Bailey, Anne M. and Josep R. Llobera, eds. 1981. The
Asiatic Mode of Production: Science and Politics.
London: Routledge and Kegan Paul.

Banks, Arthur S. 1976. Cross National Time Series:
1815-1973. Data on computer tape. Inter-university
Consortium for Political and Social Research, Ann Arbor,
Michigan.

Baran, Paul and Paul Sweezy. 1966. Monopoly Capital. New
York: Monthly Review Press.

Bell, Christopher. 1974. Portugal and the Quest for the Indies. New York: Barnes and Noble Books.

Beresford, Maurice. 1954. The Lost Villages of England. London: Lutterworth Press.

_____. 1967. New Towns of the Middle Ages: Town Plantation in England, Wales, and Gascony. New York and Washington: Fredrick A. Praeger.

_____, and John G. Hurst. eds. 1971. Deserted Medieval Villages: Studies. Guildford and London: Lutterworth Press.

Beveridge, William Henry. 1966. Prices and Wages in England: From the Twelfth to the Nineteenth Century. Volume I. Price Tables: Mercantile Era. Reprints of Economic Classics. New York: Augustus M Kelley, Bookseller.

Bingham, Christopher. 1978. "Time Series: General." International Encyclopedia of Statistics. Volume 2. Ed by W.H. Kruskal and J.M. Tanar. New York: The Free Press.

Bland, A.E., P.A. Brown, and R.H. Tawney. eds. 1914. English Economic History: Select Documents. London: G. Bell and Sons, Ltd.

Bloch, Marc. 1961. Feudal Society. Volume 1. The Growth of Ties of Dependence. Translated by L.A. Manyon. Chicago: University of Chicago Press.

Bogue, Donald. J. 1969. Principles of Demography. New York: Wiley and Sons.

Bonacich, Edna and Lucie Cheng Hirata. N.d. "Introduction: A Theoretical Orientation to International Labor Migration." Typescript photocopy.

Bowden, Peter. 1967. "Statistical Appendix." The Agrarian History of England and Wales. Volume IV, 1500-1640. General editor H.P.R. Finberg. Edited by Joan Thirsk. Cambridge: The University Press.

Braudel, F.P. 1967. "Prices in Europe from 1450 to 1750." The Economy of Expanding Europe in the Sixteenth and Seventeenth Centuries. Volume IV. Cambridge Economic History of Europe. Edited by E.E. Rich and L.H. Wilson. Cambridge: University Press.

Braverman, Harry. 1974. Labor and Monopoly Capital. New York: Monthly Review Press.

Brogan, D.W. 1967. The Development of Modern France: 1870-1939. New and revised edition. London: Hamish Hamilton.

Bromwell, William J. 1969. History of Migration to the United States Exhibiting the Number, Sex, Age, Occupation, and Country of Birth of Passangers Arriving from Foreign Countries by Sea: 1819 to 1855. Reprints of Economic Classics. New York: Augustus M. Kelley.

Brown, E.H. Phelps and Sheila V. Hopkins. 1955. "Seven Centuries of Building Wages." Economica 22, 87 (August): 195-206.

_____. 1956. "Seven Centuries of the Prices of Consumables, compared with Builders Wage-rates" Economica 23, 92 (November): 296-314.

_____. 1957. "Wage-rates and Prices: Evidence for Population Pressure in the Sixteenth Century." Economica 24, 96 (November): 289-306.

_____. 1959. "Builders Wage-rates, Prices, and Population: Some Further Evidence." Economica 26, 101 (February): 18-38.

_____. 1961. "Seven Centuries of Wages and Prices: Some Earlier Estimates." Economica 28, 104 (February): 30-36.

_____. 1981. A Perspective of Wages and Prices. London: Methuen.

Caldwell, Malcolm. 1977. The Wealth of Some Nations. London: Zed Press.

Chambers, J.D. 1972. Population, Economy, and Society in Pre-Industrial England. Edited, preface, introduction by W.A. Armstrong. London: Oxford University Press.

Chandler, Tertius and Gerald Fox. 1974. 3000 Years of Urban Growth. Foreward by Lewis Mumford. New York and London: Academic Press.

Cipolla, Carlo M. 1976. Before the Industrial Revolution: European Society and Economy, 1000-1700" New York: W.W. Norton and Company Inc.

_____. 1978. The Economic History of World Population. Seventh edition. Harmondsworth: Penguin Books.

Clapp, B.W., ed. 1976. Documents in English Economic History: England Since 1760. Document series edited by B.W. Clapp, H.E.S. Fisher, and A.R.J. Jurica. London: G.Bell and Sons.

Clarkson, L.A. 1971. The Pre-Industrial Economy in England: 1500-1750. London: B.T. Batsford Ltd.

Cole, G.D.H. 1954. Introduction to Economic History: 1750-1950. London: Macmillan and Co.

Darby, H.C., ed. 1973. A New Historical Geography of England. Cambridge: University Press.

Davis, Ralph. 1973. English Overseas Trade: 1500-1700. London: Macmillan.

Day, Richard B. 1976. "The Theory of the Long Cycles: Kondratiev, Trotsky, Mandel." New Left Review 99 (September-October): 67-82.

Deane, Phyllis and W.A. Cole. 1967 British Economic Growth, 1688-1959: Trends and Structure. Second edition. Cambridge: University Press.

Dewey, Edward R. and Edwin F. Dakin. 1947. Cycles: The Science of Prediction. New York: Henry Holt and Co.

Dike, K. Onwuka. 1956. Trade and Politics in the Niger Delta:1830-1885. Oxford: Clarenford Press.

Dobb, Maurice. 1963. Studies in the Development of Capitalism. New York: International Publishers.

_____. 1978a. "A Reply." The Transition from Feudalism to Capitalism. Edited by Rodney Hilton. London: Verso.

_____. 1978b. "A Further Comment." The Transition from Feudalism to Capitalism. Edited by Rodney Hilton. London: Verso.

_____. 1978c. "From Feudalism to Capitalism." The Transition From Feudalism to Capitalism. Edited by Rodney Hilton. London: Verso.

Dobson, R.B. 1970. The Peasant's Revolt of 1381. London: MacMillan.

Donkin, R.A. 1973. "Changes in the Early Middle Ages." A
    New Historical Geography of England. Edited by
    H.C.Darby. Cambridge: University Press.

Donnan, Elizabeth. 1930. Documents Illustrative of the
    History of the Slave Trade to America. Washington,
    D.C.: Carnegie Institution of Washington.

East, Gordon. 1966. An Historical Geography of Europe.
    London: Methuen and Co. Ltd.

Easterlin, Richard. 1968. Population, Labor Force, and
    Long Swings in Economic Growth: The American
    Experience. New York: National Bureau of Economic
    Research.

Edwards, Richard. 1979. Contested Terrain: The
    Transformation of the Workplace in the Twentieth
    Century. New York: Basic Books.

Edwards, Richard, Micheal Reich, and David M. Gordon. 1979.
    Labor Market Segmentation. Lexington, MA: D.C. Heath
    and Co.

Elliott, David L. 1978. Thailand: Origins of Military
    Rule. London: Zed Press.

Elliott, J.H. 1977. Imperial Spain: 1469-1716. New York:
    Meridian Books.

Emmanuel, Arghiri. 1972. Unequal Exchange: A Study of the
    Imperialism of Trade. Translated by Brian Pearce. New
    York: Monthly Review Press.

Ferenczi, Imre. 1929. International Migrations. Volume I
    Statistics. Edited by Walter Wilcox. New York: National
    Bureau of Economic Research.

Fischer, Ernst. 1973. Marx in His Own Words. With Franz
    Marek. Translated by Anna Bostock. Harmondsworth:
    Penguin Books.

Fox-Genovese, Elizabeth and Eugene D. Genovese. 1983.
    Fruits of Merchant Capital: Slavery and Bourgeois
    Property in the Rise and Expansion of Capitalism. New
    York: Oxford Univerity Press.

Frank, Andre Gunder. 1978. World Accumulation: 1492-1789.
    New York and London: Monthly Review Press.

Goldscheider, Calvin. 1971. Population, Modernization, and Social Structure. Boston: Little, Brown and Co.

Greenleaf, Barbara Kaye. 1970. American Fever: The Story of American Immigration. New York: Four Winds Press.

Gregg, Pauline. 1976. Black Death to Industrial Revolution: A Social and Economic History of England. New York: Barnes and Noble Books.

Hamilton Earl J. 1929. "American Treasure and the Rise of Capitalism (1500-1700)." Economica 27 (November): 338-57.

Hammarstrom, Docent Ingrid. 1957. "The 'Price Revolution' of the Sixteenth Century: Some Swedish Evidence." The Scandinavian Economic History Review 5, 1: 118-154.

Handlin, Oscar. 1959. Immigration as a Factor in American Life. Englewood Cliffs, N.J.: Prentice Hall.

Handlin, Oscar. 1973. The Uprooted. Second enlarged edition. Boston: Little, Brown and Co.

Hansen, Marcus Lee. 1961. The Atlantic Migration, 1607-1860: A History of the Continuing Settlement of the United States. Edited by Arthur M. Schlesinger. New York: Harper Torchbooks.

Hanson, Carl A. 1981. Economy and Society in Baroque Portugal: 1668-1703. Minneapolis: University of Minnesota Press.

Harris, Marvin. 1977. Cannibals and Kings: The Origins of Cultures. New York: Random House.

Helliener, Karl F. 1967. "The Population of Europe from the Black Death to the Vital Revolution." The Economy of Expanding Europe in the Sixteenth and Seventeenth Centuries. Volume IV. Cambridge Economc History of Europe. Edited by E.E. Rich and L.H. Wilson. Cambridge: University Press.

Hill, Christopher. 1948. "The English Civil War Interpreted by Marx and Engels." Science and Society. 12, 1 (Winter): 130-56.

_____. 1969. Reformation to Industrial Revolution, 1530-1780. The Pelican Economic History of Britain: Volume 2. London: Penguin Books.

Hillgarth, J.N. 1978. The Spanish Kingdoms. Volume II.
Oxford: Clarendon Press.

Hilton, Rodney. 1949. "Peasant Movements in England Before
1381." The Economic History Review Second series, 2, 2:
117-136.

_____. 1973. Bond Men Made Free: Medieval Peasant
Movements and the English Rising of 1381. New York: The
Viking Press.

_____, ed. 1978. The Transition From Feudalism to
Capitalism. Introduction by Rodney Hilton. London:
Verso.

Hindress, Barry and Paul Q. Hirst. 1975. Pre-Capitalist
Modes of Production. London: Routledge and Kegen Paul.

_____. 1977. Mode of Production and Social Formation: An
Auto-Critique of Pre-Capitalist Modes of Production.
Atlantic Highlands, N.J.: Humanities Press.

History Task Force. 1979. Labor Migration Under
Capitalism: The Puerto Rican Experience. Centro de
Estudios Puertorriquenos. New York: Monthly Review
Press.

Hobsbawm, E.J. 1954a.. "The General Crisis of the European
Economy in the 17th Century." Past and Present 5 (May):
33-53.

_____. 1954b. "The Crisis of the 17th Century--II." Past
and Present 6 (November): 44-65.

_____. 1960. "The Seventeenth Century in the Development
of Capitalism." Science and Society 24, 2: 97-112.

_____. 1977. The Age of Revolution: Europe 1789-1848.
London: Sphere Books.

Hobson, J. A. 1972. Imperialism. University of Michigan:
Ann Arbor Paperbacks.

Hoskins, W. G. 1976. The Age of Plunder, King Henry's
England: 1500-1547. London and New York: Longman.

Hubbert, M. King. 1962. Energy Resources. A Report to the
Committee on Natural Resources of the National Academy
of Sciences--National Research Council. Publication
1000-D. Washington, D.C.: National Academy of
Sciences--National Research Council.

Imlah, Albert. 1958. Economic Elements in the Pax
   Britannica: Studies in British Foreign Trade in the
   Nineteenth Century. Cambridge, Ma.: Harvard University
   Press.

Immigration Commission. 1911a. Abstracts of the Reports of
   the Immigration Commission. Volume II. 61st Congress,
   3rd Sesion, U.S. Senate, Document No. 747. Washington,
   D.C.: Government Printing Office.

_____. 1911b. Statistical Review of Immigration,
   1820-1910: Distribution of Immigrants, 1850-1900. 61st
   Congress, U.S. Senate, Document No. 756. Washington,
   D.C.: Government Printing Office.

Isard, W. 1942a. "A Neglected Cycle: The Transport
   Building Cycle." Review of Economic Statistics 24, 4
   (November): 149-58.

_____. 1942b. "Transport Development and Building Cycles."
   Quarterly Journal of Economics 57, 4 (Novmber): 90-112.

Jack, Sybil M. 1977. Trade and Industry in Tudor and
   Stuart England. London: George Allen and Unwin Ltd.

Jackson, T. A. 1973. Ireland Her Own: An Outline History
   of the Irish Struggle for National Freedom and
   Independence. Edited and epilogue by C. Desmond
   Greaves. Berlin: Seven Seas Publishers.

Jerome, Harry. 1926. Migration and Business Cycles. New
   York: NBER.

Johnson, Stanley C. 1913. A History of Emigration: From
   the United Kingdom to North America, 1763-1912. London:
   George Routledge and Sons.

Johnston, J. 1972. Econometric Methods. Second edition.
   New York: McGraw-Hill Book Co.

Jusserand, J. J. 1889. English Wayfaring Life in the
   Middle Ages. Translated by Lucy Toulmin Smith. London:
   Ernest Benn Limited.

Kiernan, V.G. 1966. The Revolution of 1854 in Spanish
   History. Oxford: Clarendon Press.

Kondratieff, N. D. 1978. "The Long Waves in Economic
   Life." Lloyds Bank Review 129 (July): 41-60.

Krader, Lawrence. 1975. The Asiatic Mode of Production: Sources, Development, and Critique in the Writings of Karl Marx. Assem, The Netherlands: Van Gorcum and Co.

Kritz, Mary M., Charles B. Keely and Silvano M. Tomasi, ed. 1981. Global Trends in Migration. New York: Center for Migration Studies.

Kuznets, Simon. 1930. Secular Movements in Production and Prices. Boston: Houghton Mifflin.

_____. 1961. Capital in the American Economy: Its Formation and Financing. Princeton: University Press.

_____, and Ernest Rubin. 1954. Immigration and the Foreign Born. Occasional Paper 46. New York: NBER.

Lee, Everett S. 1966. "A Theory of Migration." Demography 3, 1: 47-57.

Lenin, V. I. 1970. Imperialism: The Highest Stage of Capitalism. Scientific Socialism Series. Moscow: Progress Publishers.

Magdoff, Harry. 1969. The Age of Imperialism: The Economics of U.S. Foreign Policy. New York: Modern Reader Paperbacks.

Maldonado-Denis, Manuel. 1980. The Immigration Dialectic: Puerto Rico and U.S.A. New York: International Publishers.

Mandel, Ernest. 1978. Late Capitalism. London: Verso.

Mangalam, J.J. and Harry K Schwarzweller. 1970. "Some Theoretical Guidelines Toward a Sociology of Migration." International Migration Review 4, 2 (Spring): 5-21.

Mannix, Daniel P. and Malcom Cowley. 1962. Black Cargoes: A History of the Atlantic Slave Trade, 1518-1865. New York: Viking Press.

Marques, A.H. de Oliveira. 1971. Daily Life in Portugul in the Late Middle Ages. Translated by S.S. Wyatt. Madison: The University of Wisconsin Press.

Marx, Karl. 1939. Revolution in Spain. Marxist Library, Works of Marxism-Leninism. Volume XII. New York: International Publishers.

_____. 1946. Capital. Volume I. Dona Torr edition. London: George Allen and Unwin.

_____. 1964. Pre-Capitalist Economic Forms. Translated by Jack Cohen. Edited by Eric J. Hobsbawm. New York: International Publishers.

_____. 1968. Theories of Surplus Value. Part III. Moscow: Progress Publishers.

_____. 1973. Surveys from Exile: Political Writings. Volume 2. Edited by David Fernbach. Harmondsworth: Penguin Books.

Matras, Judah. 1977. Introduction to Population: A Sociological Approach. Englewood Cliffs, N. J.: Prentice-Hall.

Nabudere, Dan Wadada. 1977. The Political Economy of Imperialism. London: Zed Press.

Olsson, Gunnar. 1965. Distance and Human Migration: A Review and Bibliography. Bibliography Series Number Two. Philadelphia: Regional Science Research Institute.

Outhwaite, R.B. 1969. Inflation in Tudor and Early Stuart England. London: Macmillan.

Park, Robert E. 1928. "Human Migration and the Marginal Man." American Journal of Sociology 33, 6 (May): 881-93.

Peterson, William. 1969. Population. Second edition. London: Macmillan.

Phythian-Adams, Charles. 1978. "Urban Decay in Late Medieval England." Towns in Society: Essays in Economic History and Historical Sociology. Edited by Philip Abrams and E.A. Wrigley. Cambridge: Cambridge University Press.

Pindyck, Robert S. and Daniel L Rubinfeld. 1981. Econometric Models and Economic Forecasts. Second edition. New York: McGraw-Hill Book Co.

Piore, Michael J. 1979. Birds of Passage: Migrant Labor and Industrial Societies. Cambridge: Cambridge University Press.

Pirenne, Henri. 1952. Medieval Cities: Their Origins and the Revival of Trade. Translated by Frank D. Halsey. Princeton, N. J.: Princeton University Press.

Post, Ken. 1978. Arise Ye Starvelings: The Jamaican Labour Rebellion of 1938 and its Aftermath. Institute of Social Studies Series on the Development of Societies. Volume III. The Hague: Martinus Nijhoff.

President's Science Advisory Committee. 1967. The World Food Problem: Report of the Panel on the World Food Supply. Volume II. May. Washington, D.C.: The White House.

Raftis, J. Ambrose. 1964. Tenure and Mobility: Studies in the Social History of the Mediaeval English Village. Toronto: Pontifical Institute of Mediaeval Studies.

Ravenstein, E. G. 1885. "The Laws of Migration." Journal of the Royal Statistical Society, 48 (June): 167-227.

_____. 1889. "The Laws of Migration." Part II. Journal of the Royal Statistical Society, 52 (June): 241-301.

Rich, E.E. 1967. "Colonial Settlement and its Labour Problems." The Economy of Expanding Europe in the Sixteenth and Seventeenth Centuries. Volume IV. Cambridge Economc History of Europe. Edited by E.E. Rich and L.H. Wilson. Cambridge: University Press.

Rodney, Walter. 1967. West Africa and the Atlantic Slave Trade. Nairobi: East African Publishing House.

Rostow, W. W. 1980. Why the Poor Get Rich and the Rich Slow Down. Austin: University of Texas Press.

Rothstein, Richard. 1975. "The Urban Ethnic Working Class." Green Mountain Quarterly. 1 (November): 1-24.

Russell, Josiah Cox. 1948. British Medieval Population. Albuquerque: Univesity of New Mexico Press.

Schumpeter, Joseph A. 1939. Business Cycles: A Theoretical, Historical, and Statistical Analysis of the Capitalist Process. Volume I. First edition. New York: McGraw-Hill Book Company.

Schade, Louis. 1856. The Immigration into the United States of America, from a Statistical and National-Economic Point of View. Washington: Printed at the Union Office.

Shaw, R. Paul. 1975. Migration Theory and Fact: A Review and Bibliography of Current Literature. Bibliography Series Number Five. Philadelphia: Regional Science Research Institute.

SAS. 1982. SAS/ETS User's Guide. 1982 edition. Cary, North Carolina: SAS Institute, Inc.

Simeral, Margaret. 1978. "Women and the Reserve Army of Labor." Insurgent Sociologist , 8, 2 and 3.

Simon, Julian, ed. 1978. Research in Population Economics: An Annual Compilation of Research. Volume I. Greenwich, CN: JAI Press.

Sjoberg, Gideon. 1960. The Preindustrial City: Past and Present. New York: The Free Press.

Smith, C. T. 1967. An Historical Geography of Western Europe Before 1800. New York: Fredrick A. Praeger.

Standing, Guy. 1981. "Migration and Modes of Exploitation: Social Origins of Immobility and Mobility." Journal of Peasant Studies 8,2: 173-211.

Sweezy, Paul. 1978a. "A Critique." The Transition from Feudalism to Capitalism. Edited by Rodney Hilton. London: Verso.

_____. 1978b. "A Rejoinder." The Transition from Feudalism to Capitalism. Edited by Rodney Hilton. London: Verso.

Szymanski, Albert. 1981. The Logic of Imperialism. New York: Praeger.

Tilly, Charles. 1975. "Food Supply and Public Order in Modern Europe." Charles Tilly, editor. The Formation of Nation States in Western Europe. Princeton: Princeton University Press.

_____. 1981 As Sociology Meets History. New York: Academic Press.

Thirsk, Joan and J.P. Cooper. 1972. Seventeenth Century Economic Documents. Oxford: Clarendon Press.

Thomas, Brinley. 1954. Migration and Economic Growth: A Study of Great Britain and the Atlantic Economy. Cambridge: Cambridge University Press.

_____. 1973. Migration and Economic Growth: A Study of Great Britain and the Atlantic Economy. Second edition. Cambridge: Cambridge University Press.

Thomas, Dorothy Swaine. 1927. Social Aspects of the Business Cycle. New York: Alfred A. Knopf.

Thomas, W. I. and Florian Znaniecki. 1918-1920. The Polish Peasant in Europe and America. 5 Volumes. Boston: R.G. Badger.

Thompson, E.P. 1966. The Making of the English Working Class. New York: Vintage Books.

Thomson, David, ed. 1968. France: Empire and Republic, 1850-1940, Historical Documents. New York: Walker and Co.

United States Immigration and Naturalization Service. 1978. Statistical Yearbook. Washington, D.C.: U.S. Government Printing Office.

Usher, Abbott Payson. 1931. "Prices of Wheat and Commodity Price Indexes for England, 1259-1930." Review of Economic Statistics 13, 1 (February): 103-113.

Uslaner, E.M. 1978. "Editor's Introduction." Time Series Analysis: Regression Techniques. By Charles W. Ostrom, Jr. Series: Quantitative Applications in the Social Sciences. Sage University Paper. Beverly Hills: Sage Publications.

Valentey, D. I. 1980. An Outline Theory of Population. Moscow: Progress Publishers.

Vance, Rupert B. 1952. "Is Theory for Demographers?" Social Forces 31 (October): 9-13.

Wachter, Kenneth W., Eugene A. Hammel and Peter Laslett. 1978. Statistical Studies of Historical Social Structure. New York: Academic Press.

Wallerstein, Immanuel. 1974. The Modern World-System I: Capitalist Agriculture and the Origins of the European World-Economy in the Sixteenth Century. New York: Academic Press.

Walvin, James. 1982. Slavery and British Society: 1776-1846. Baton Rouge: Louisiana State University Press.

Wander, Hilde. 1979. "Future Prospects of Magnitude and Trends of International Migration." Prospects of Population: Methodology and Assumptions. Papers of the Ad Hoc Group of Experts on Demographic Projections, United Nations Headquarters, November 7-11, 1977. Department of International Economic and Social Affairs, Population Studies, No. 67. New York: United Nations.

Weber, Max. 1976. "The Nature of the City." Paul Meadows and Ephraim H. Mizruchi, editors. Urbanism, Urbanization, and Change: Comparative Perspectives. Second edition. Reading, Massachusetts: Addison-Wesley Publishing Company.

Weber, Robert Philip. 1981. "Society and Economy in the Western World System." Social Forces 59, 4 (June): 1130-1148.

Williams, Eric. 1966. Capitalism and Slavery. New York: Capricorn Books, G.P. Putnam's Sons.

Willaimson, Jeffery G. 1964. American Growth and the Balance of Payments: 1820-1913: A Study of the Long Swing. Chapel Hill: University of North Carolina Press.

Wrigley, E. A. 1969. Population and History. World University Library. New York: McGraw-Hill Book Company.

DATE

NOV 1 5 1994

OCT 23 1995

MAR 1 9 1996

APR 2 5 1996

MAR 1 1 1997

FEB 1 5 1998

Printed
in USA